All
Made
Up

All Made Up

A Girl's Guide

to Seeing Through

Celebrity Hype . . .

and Celebrating *Real* Beauty

Audrey D. Brashich

Illustrations by Shawn Banner

WALKER & COMPANY NEW YORK

First published in the United States of America in 2006 by
Walker Publishing Company, Inc.
Distributed to the trade by Holtzbrinck Publishers

For information about permission to reproduce selections from
this book, write to Permissions, Walker & Company,
104 Fifth Avenue, New York, New York 10011.

Library of Congress Cataloging-in-Publication Data

Brashich, Audrey.
All made up : a girl's guide to seeing through celebrity hype and celebrating
real beauty / Audrey Brashich ; illustrations by Shawn Banner.
p. cm.
Includes bibliographical references.
ISBN-10: 0-8027-7744-9 · ISBN-13: 978-0-8027-7744-7 (paperback)
ISBN-10: 0-8027-8074-1 · ISBN-13: 978-0-8027-8074-4 (hardcover)
1. Girls—Psychology. 2. Girls—Attitudes. 3. Beauty, Personal. 4. Girls in
popular culture. 5. Self-perception in adolescence. 6. Body image in
adolescence. I. Banner, Shawn. II. Title.
HQ777.B63 2006   305.235'2—dc22   2005037183

Book design by Chris Welch

Visit Walker & Company's Web site at www.walkeryoungreaders.com

Printed in the United States of America

2   4   6   8   10   9   7   5   3   1

All papers used by Walker & Company are natural, recyclable products made
from wood grown in well-managed forests. The manufacturing processes
conform to the environmental regulations of the country of origin.

For my husband, Chris, who made it possible for me to
write this book and believed in it from the start.
And for my parents, Catherine Sidor and Deyan Brashich,
who sent me everywhere I needed to go.
—A. B.

To my media-savvy children, Isaac and Rosalie, who love books
and love that I illustrate them; and to my mom, who has
always looked beyond media-promoted images to
find what's truly beautiful.
—S. B.

Thank you

Eva Ingvarson (Captain, Team *All Made Up*) and Alan Albert, Michaela Albert, Talia Albert, Liz Bakulski, Shawn Banner, Ran Barton, Lori Berger, Mindy Bingham, Wendy Bingham, Heather Blaine, Meghan Boone, Camilla Bradley, Jan Cohn, John H. Chatfield, Thomas Cooper, Frank Couvares, Megan Curren, Ara Cusack, Chandra Czape, Catherine Dee, Emily Easton, Ariel Fox, Helen Friedman, Kim Goldstein, Lori Gottlieb, Kris Gowen, GoVeg.Com, Nancy Gruver, Frank Habbas, Gina Breuer Hadley, Elaine Henizman, Carolyn B. Heller, Richard Hersh, Nicolas Imhof, Lisa Jervis, Jackson Katz, Christina Kelly, Kristen Kemp, Jean Kilbourne, Gail O'Connor, Yi Shun Lai, Jennifer Lamm, Ali Laputka, Christof Laputka, Jesse Leary, Margo Maine, Billy Mann, Birgitte Mann, Tyler Merson, Mary Elizabeth Michaels, Alexis Brashich Morledge, Alison Muh, Teresa Niven, Kendra Olson Hodgson, Jonathan Pearce, Jan Phillips, Krista Reiner, Alison C. Ross, Lara Ross, Atoosa Rubenstein, Eric Sanders, Lise Sanders, Susan Schulz, Regan Otto Schroeder, Arielle Shapiro, Duncan Smith, Tamara Sobel, Douglas Starr, Kate Sullivan, Leora Tanenbaum, Malissa Thompson, Caroline Ticarro-Parker, Tim Travaglini, Rory Valentine, Beth Walker, Jessica Weiner, Louis Wikström, David Winer, Rob Williams, Lisa Wren, Anna Yie, Gemma Yie, Dina Zeckhausen, Andi Zeisler—and to the many teens who shared their candid, important opinions with me.

Contents

I Believed the Hype

I have a confession: I used to be starstruck. Really, *really* starstruck. I didn't obsessively collect celebrities' autographs or make scrapbooks full of their photos. But I did wholeheartedly buy into the definitions of female beauty and success hyped by the media. Growing up, I believed that models were the most beautiful and successful women in the world. I knew everything about them: whom they dated, which agencies represented them, how they got discovered, which products they supposedly used, and where they shopped. I regularly spent my entire allowance on magazines, model exercise videos, and makeup guides—plus the inside of my locker was covered with model photos and quotations. Since I thought they symbolized beauty and success, I even persuaded my parents to send me to an expensive seminar run by a modeling agent, where I hoped to learn how to be the next supermodel. And when shopping for clothes, I wouldn't even *look* at something that I didn't think they would wear.

Back then, I couldn't name a woman who had won a Nobel Prize or a female doctor making strides toward curing cancer or AIDS. I didn't know about female artists whose works hang in New York and Paris museums or successful businesswomen, either. The magazines I read and TV shows I watched didn't mention them—and I never bothered to wonder why. Fashion models were my role models. They were adored worldwide and reportedly didn't get out of bed for less than $10,000 a day. More importantly, they epitomized the look that was considered beautiful, and because of that they seemed to have a better lifestyle than women who didn't. I believed if I could just get discovered and maybe a little famous that I'd be considered beautiful and successful, too, and get all the money, fame, power, attention, perks, and preferential treatment models seemed to enjoy.

When I was in tenth grade, *Seventeen* magazine happened to hold a model audition at my high school in New York City. I thought it might be my big break, so I stood in line with just about every one of my female schoolmates, who were probably dreaming, as I was, about how getting chosen might change the rest of their lives. The magazine's staff had taken over the principal's office, and once inside I posed awkwardly

for a few instant photos and gushed about how badly I
wanted to be a model, how it was my lifelong dream,
and so on. The editors were pretty unmoved by my en-
thusiasm, but then they probably saw wannabes like me
every day.

A few weeks later, *Seventeen* called to tell me I had
been chosen to model for a spring fashion spread. No
one else from my school had been selected, and I could

sense some jealousy from female classmates, but I didn't let it derail me from my goal of becoming a model, which I thought would prove I was pretty and successful. At the shoot, the editors dressed me in a cheesy green windbreaker, yellow Capri pants, red-and-white striped socks, white gloves with red polka-dots, and quilted sneakers. It was a horrendous getup that no one in her right mind would ever be caught dead wearing—except for me, I guess. *That's* how badly I wanted to be a model.

After the *Seventeen* gig, I had a few other experiences that really made me feel like I was on my way. When I applied to college, the admissions application asked for a photo to be attached. Without really thinking about what it might be used for, I sent a head shot from my modeling portfolio, where I had been made up by a professional makeup artist (no visible zits!), shot at my best angle (to hide the bump in my nose!), and had red-carpet-perfect hair. Let's just say it wasn't like most of the other snapshots submitted for the fresh-man Face Book, which was where the application photos ended up the following autumn. When I arrived on campus, I felt like a star because everywhere I went (the dining hall, the laundry room, the welcome cookout on the quad), I kept overhearing people whisper things like, "I think she's a model! Did you see her photo in the Face Book?" I hadn't even unpacked and was getting invited to parties with senior guys because they'd heard I modeled. It was everything I had dreamed of, and I felt like the next Kate, Naomi, Claudia, Cindy, or Gisele. . . .

By now, you're probably wondering why I'm telling you all this. Well, it's because even as I worked toward my dream, I had experiences that made me question why models, stars, "It" girls, and other celebrities are often more famous and admired than other accomplished women. Sure, it was cool to be in *Seventeen* and to get a few compliments from some of my classmates for looking cute in the photos. But a few snapshots in a magazine wasn't nearly as important as being one of the first girls elected to my high school's student government in its almost three-hundred-year history. (It was founded in 1709!) But that honor didn't make me more desirable or cool. And it made me wonder why.

The way some guys bought into the hype about models, stars, and celebrities also made me think hard about which women are celebrated as ideals. One summer, I modeled some J. Crew clothes for the *New York Times,* and I hoped that David, a model who was representing Abercrombie & Fitch, would ask me out even

though he had totally ignored me when mutual friends had introduced us a few weeks earlier. Unfortunately, my wish came true. After realizing that I was a model, David pestered me for months to go out with him. It was like the label "model" made me more attractive or worthy of dating in his opinion, and that was absolutely not OK. Because even though I wanted to be considered model-gorgeous, I wanted to be liked for more than my appearance or because I had a certain job. I definitely didn't want to date a "modelizer," who cared more about looks and a label than anything else. So as cute as David was, I turned him down because it was clear that he didn't like me for *me* at all.

My guy friends in college were even worse. When a girl we sort of knew (I'll call her Emma) announced she was going off to Paris to model for the summer, they immediately started acting like they were best friends with Emma, and "casually" mentioned every chance they got that Emma had spoken to them directly about her summer plans and that she intended to keep in touch with them from Europe. The guys all wanted to make it seem like they weren't impressed by the fact that Emma was a model, but it was obvious that her boost in popularity was directly connected to her summer job. Meanwhile, these same guys barely congratulated our close girlfriends on their amazing summer jobs as a lab assistant for a world-renowned doctor and an intern at a prestigious Wall Street investment bank—jobs for which there had been lots of tough intellectual and academic competition. It was so backward! I mean, I thought modeling was cool, too, but those other jobs and girls deserved at least equal praise and attention.

Another thing that changed my thinking was realizing how much work it takes to achieve the look that's considered beautiful. Back in middle school and high school, I was a competitive ice skater and so naturally thin that my coach actually pestered me constantly to *gain* weight. While other athletes at the rink were subsisting on nothing more than tomatoes and cottage cheese, my coach sent me to McDonald's every day for a Big Mac. Now, I'm not complaining—I know I was lucky, but around the same time a photographer who did some test shots for my modeling portfolio told me that I'd have to do some "serious sit-ups" to lose weight if I was going to make it. I thought he was

joking, since my coach insisted I bulk up, but the photographer honestly thought I needed to slim down. Looking back, I guess I should have thanked him, because his comments made me realize how extreme and unrealistic the popular conception of beauty is—and how much time I would have had to dedicate to getting it.

But what really turned me around was discovering that I was not the only girl who had been influenced by all the hype about models, stars, "It" girls, and celebrities. After college, I became an intern and later an editor at several teen magazines, then I started my own Web community that explored why some women are celebrated by the media while others are virtually ignored—and I was amazed by the thousands of letters, e-mails, and posts from girls who wrote in asking about how they could look like—or become—models, stars, or world-famous celebrities. They sent snapshots of themselves in bikinis and talked about quitting their favorite sports teams so they wouldn't get injuries that could affect their appearance. They wrote about starving themselves and told me things like:

"I don't know if you can help me, but I want to start a modeling career. I have already spent thousands of dollars on John Casablancas School of Modeling." —Cassie, 19

"My dream has always been to model. I have taken Glamour Shots . . . if you believe that you can help me, please let me know." —Anonymous, 15

"I am twelve years old, and I want to be a singer more than anything the world has to offer." —Charissa, 12

Talk about "Been there, done that"! Reading those letters was like reliving my own past dreams. I knew *exactly* what these girls were feeling. They believed that stars, models, and "It" girls symbolize beauty and success—just like I once did. And that made me realize that media moguls, advertisers, and manufacturers have a lot of control over what gets seen and what's available to buy. I noticed that they generally only celebrate women who help sell the products and services they create. Then they act like those women are the most beautiful and successful and reward them with status and media attention—which makes us want to be like them. In other words, they deliberately make us starstruck.

Today I no longer believe all the hype. That doesn't mean I don't surf the Web, read gossip magazines at the grocery store checkout, or wait in line to see the newest blockbuster. I *absolutely* do all of that. Who doesn't?! I just no longer accept that the symbols of beauty and success hyped by the media are the best—or only—ones out there. Instead, I try to seek out more diverse, inspiring, *real* role models and decide for myself who I think is beautiful and what I consider successful—and you can do that, too.

BACK TALK BLOG

Head to allmadeup.net to post your thoughts about celebrity hype and real beauty on the Back Talk Blog. Get started with these questions:

☆ Who do you think decides what's beautiful and who's successful?

☆ How do you define beauty and success?

☆ Why do you think stars, models, and other celebrities are the most celebrated women in the world?

chapter two

Models, Stars, and Celebrities

ashion models, Hollywood starlets, pop stars, reality TV personalities, and *celebutantes* (well-born party girls famous mostly for their family names and wealth)—they're everywhere, from magazine covers to posters at bus stops. They star in reality TV programs, have official Web sites, and design clothing lines. Perfumes, cosmetics, and clubs are named after them, and gossip blogs report on their romances and pregnancies. They're the most recognizable women on the planet, while women who work to make the world a better place are pretty much invisible. Why?

The Rise of the Supermodel

Modeling Milestones

Models haven't always been icons of beauty and success. In fact, they used to be considered low class and frequently compared to prostitutes. This time line charts some important moments in their evolution from rock bottom to role model.

1920s

☆ John Robert Powers opens the world's first modeling agency in New York City. By the mid-1930s, it represents over 500 models, whom many consider "empty-headed floozies."

☆ The first model search contest is held, but many models use only their first name in order to remain anonymous, since modeling was then considered disreputable.

1930s

☆ Most models earn $25 per week. Some earn up to $75 or $100.

☆ Twiggy, a seventeen-year-old Brit who weighs ninety-one pounds, is named "the Face of '66" by an English newspaper. Her body is cast for shop-window mannequins, and she launches a stocking line, a hairdressing salon, and a hip boutique, making her modeling's first international star.

1940s **1950s** **1960s**

☆ Clyde Matthew Dessner, the owner of a small modeling agency, coins the term *supermodel*.

☆ "Model hounds," men who aspire to date models because of their status, appear.

☆ In England, models start to become accepted into society. Some marry well-established politicians and aristocrats.

☆ A British modeling agency called English Boy (representing mostly women) calls its clients "not just models, but model people—models for other people to model themselves on."

●●●●●●● 1960s ●●●●●● 1970s ●●●●●●●●●●●●●●●●●●●●●●●●

☆ Models and rock stars become famous for their wild parties and personalities. They start to become international stars and celebrities.

☆ John Casablancas establishes Elite Model Management, a modeling agency that later helps catapult Stephanie Seymour, Naomi Campbell, Cindy Crawford, and Linda Evangelista to superstardom.

☆ Cheryl Tiegs, an American model from California who had modeled for *Seventeen, Glamour,* and *Teen,* earns $2,000 for a day's work. In 1979, she inks a deal with Cover Girl for $1.5 million over five years.

☆ Ford Models launches the "Face of the '80s," an international model competition later known as the "Supermodel of the World" event.

☆ *Paper Dolls,* a made-for-TV movie and later a series, depicts young models living a dream life in New York City.

☆ Naomi Campbell, Linda Evangelista, Christy Turlington shoot to the top of the modeling profession, appearing in fashion spreads, flying first class, and staying in the finest hotels.

☆ Claudia Schiffer is discovered in a German disco and later becomes the top paid model of the 1990s, earning about $10 million a year.

☆ The hippest, sexiest video on MTV is George Michael's song "Freedom," which stars Cindy, Christy, Linda, Naomi, and others instead of lesser known actresses or models.

● ●●●● **1980s** ●●●● ●●●●●●● ●●●●●● **1990s** ●●●●●●●●●●

☆ A Blockbuster video television commercial features a dumpy guy snagging the last copy of a new release for his wife but giving it away to Cindy Crawford because he's so starstruck.

☆ *Top Model,* a bi-monthly magazine dedicated to gossip and information about models, launches.

☆ *Models Inc.,* a drama about the life of models behind the cameras and beyond the runways, becomes a TV series.

☆ Modeling fans and tourists flock to the first Fashion Cafe in NYC, which is partially owned by Naomi Campbell, Claudia Schiffer, Elle Macpherson, and Christy Turlington.

☆ *Time* magazine runs an article titled, "The Fall of the Supermodel," which argues that fashion designers and the public are tired of models' prima donna attitudes and demands— yet models continue to reign.

●○●○○○○ **1990S** ○○●○○○○○○○○ ○○○○○○○○ ○○○○○○○○○○○○○○

☆ Supermodels Heidi Klum and Elle Macpherson play themselves on *Saturday Night Live, Friends,* and *Spin City.* The shows' male characters boast about dating them in front of other female characters, making it seem like models are more valuable and desirable than other women.

☆ Fashion magazines begin to feature actresses and other celebrities on their covers, blurring the line between model and star.

☆ The Victoria's Secret fashion show broadcast on the Web logs a record 1.5 million visitors and crashes the company's Web site.

☆ Modeling chat clubs with names like "The Future Victoria's Secret Models Club" flood teen Web sites.

☆ Teen magazines carry ads for Ultra Model, "The Model Search board game that gives you a taste of life as a supermodel" and an application to a local modeling agency or school that offers courses—for a fee.

2000 and Beyond

☆ The *Wall Street Journal* reports that financially struggling families in Brazil are selling their family farms in order to send their daughters to a modeling program run by the agent who discovered Gisele Bundchen.

☆ *America's Next Top Model* hits TV.

☆ *Vogue* magazine features nine models on the cover of the September 2004 issue proclaiming "The Return of the Supermodel."

○ ○ ● ○ ● ○ ● ○ **2000 and Beyond** ○ ○ ○ ○ ● ○ ○ ○ ○ ○ ○ ○ ● ○ ○ ● ○ ○ ● ○ ○ ○ ○ ● ● ○ ○ ● ○ ●

☆ NBC airs the *Sports Illustrated Swimsuit Model Search*, which features twelve women competing for a million-dollar modeling contract and the chance to appear in the magazine's annual Swimsuit Issue.

☆ The April 2005 cover of *Vanity Fair* magazine features the "new wave of eastern European supermodels."

☆ Twiggy, the 1960s' most famous model, joins *America's Next Top Model* as a judge.

What will be next?

It Pays to Look Good

In the late 1980s, winners of the Miss America pageant earned $150,000 plus a $42,000 scholarship and a car worth $30,000. A few years earlier, the average salary for women working full-time year-round was only $14,780, making being beautiful a better business for women than most other work. In fact, fashion modeling and prostitution are the only careers in which women consistently earn more money than men.

There have always been beautiful women and professions based on appearance. Over the centuries, models have posed for works of art, and for nearly a hundred years, Hollywood stars have defined glamour. But until recently, women outside these occupations weren't expected—and didn't try—to look as good as those in the public eye.

Since entering the workforce in large numbers during the Second World War, women have made real progress toward financial independence and power. Starting in the 1950s, more young women began attending college and, later, law, business, and medical schools. In fact, between 1960 and 1990, the number of female judges, lawyers, doctors, engineers, and elected officials exploded. As a result, women started competing with men for jobs and promotions in fields that were previously off-limits.

Starting in the 1980s, women (and increasingly girls) became pressured to live up to perfectionist standards of beauty. At the same time that they were headed for the top in many fields that were previously dominated by men, they became expected to spend more time, energy, and money than ever on appearance, which gave women less time to spend on making it to the top. It was as if the cultural obsession with women's appearance developed as a way to prevent women from gaining too much power and success. Of course, advertisers, manufacturers, and corporations

fully supported the connection between appearance and success because it assured them of huge profits and endless sales of wrinkle creams, hair and skin dyes, new fashions, exercise DVDs, diet books, and magazines. Plus, as fashion made a comeback from the ultracasual styles of the 1970s, the world became obsessed with

Star Treatment

Today's celebrities are treated like royalty. When presenting at awards shows, they receive goodie bags of complimentary gifts, filled with such perks as lifetime AOL memberships, Adidas sportswear, Coach accessories, Surly Girl purses, Tommy Hilfiger clothing, and Canon electronics. Rumor has it that before Jennifer Lopez arrives at a performance or on set, she demands her dressing room have white flowers, white tables and tablecloths, white candles, and white couches. Actress Sharon Stone will reportedly agree to do a movie only after filmmakers agree to her five-page list of perks, which includes Pilates equipment, a chauffeured car, three nannies, two assistants, cell phones, pagers, a presidential suite, first-class travel (if a private jet is unavailable), and a chef. Stone also gets to keep the clothing and jewelry she wears in a movie.

high style and glamour—and models became the new ideal.

The women who met these strict beauty standards became world famous. They became supermodels. Cindy Crawford, Naomi Campbell, Linda Evangelista, Claudia Schiffer, Christy Turlington, Elle Macpherson, and others shot to fame primarily because they were (and still are) tall, thin, and impeccably groomed. They became A-list celebrities and attended ultrachic parties, wore expensive clothes, and vacationed at deluxe resorts. Where they ate, whom they dated, what they wore when they weren't working, which beauty salons and personal trainers they favored all became common knowledge and sometimes even front-page news. There had probably never been more famous or recognizable women.

The Death of the Supermodel

In the late 1990s, a backlash started against the high salaries and demanding attitudes of top models. Editors were tired of dealing with them, and the public seemed to have had enough of their flashy images and over-the-top glamour. The fashion industry reflected this by favoring simpler styles and plainer models, and turning to Hollywood actresses, who seemed to have relearned some glamour from all the model mania. As a result, the impossibly perfect look embodied by the supermodels seemed like it might fade away as other stars moved into the spotlight. Unfortunately, that's not what happened. Instead of making definitions of success and beauty more real, other female celebrities started conforming to the model look.

In the Shadow of the Supermodels

All of this hype has left a lot of girls (like, ahem, yours truly) starstruck. They see the status and rewards heaped on models, stars, and "It" girls and equate it with beauty and success, which they want for themselves. See for yourself in these quotes from real girls.

"I wanna do more commercial and print-ads but I'm only thirteen.... I WANT TO BE THE NEXT SUPERMODEL!" —Lifeislikelove14, 13

"I want to be on the cover of a magazine to rub it in to all the people who hated me and for all the publicity." —Kathy, 18

"I know that it would be great if I made a difference in the world, but I want to be a model really really bad." —Kayla, 14

"I always put on a big smile whenever I go out because you never know who could be looking at you. Being discovered would be a dream come true." —Sarah, 17

"I've always wanted to model even if it meant risking my health. When I turn eighteen, I'm probably going to try modeling again and starve myself because it means that much to me." —Stacy, 16

"Modeling is on my mind every day. It's my dream. When I wake up, I run two miles, and at night I do seventy-five sit-ups to be able to stay in shape." —Amanda, 18

"I would drop whatever I'm doing to become a supermodel." —Yodith, 19

"I've wanted to be famous my whole life! I pray for it every day. Please help me get famous!" —*Clarissa, 13*

"The coolest thing about modeling is that you get a lot of attention from people, and they seem to like you more." —*Carly, 13*

Dreamers and Wannabes

Over 8,000 hopefuls auditioned for the second season of Tyra Banks's reality competition *America's Next Top Model*. Large model conventions typically draw 2,000 to 2,500 contestants and 200 agencies, while smaller ones range from 800 to 1,000 contestants.

The Truth Behind the Hype

There's no doubt that being a model, star, or "It" girl would make for an exciting existence. First-class travel, sophisticated people, fancy events, adoring fans . . . but that's not the whole story. There are plenty of disadvantages—they just don't get much publicity because they'd shatter the fantasy created by the media and manufacturers to keep us buying their products (more on that in chapter 3). Some of the downsides are:

> **No Privacy** Celebrities are trailed en route to doctors' offices and the gym. Their trash is picked through, and their private moments (romantic weddings, passionate arguments, new babies, heart-wrenching breakups) are ruined by

paparazzi and fanatical stalkers. Even their private home videos (ahem, Paris) end up for sale. What they probably wouldn't give to be able to leave the house in some old sweats and with bad hair.

Dishonest "Friends" Stars have to worry about whether their best friends are going to sell their innermost secrets or keep their lips sealed when supermarket tabloids flash the cash. And new guys? Fuhgeddaboudit. Impossible to know if they're sincere or starstruck. Then there's the problem of money managers who steal while supposedly "safeguarding" celebs' investments. Who can be trusted?

Body Obsession In the grand scheme of things, perfect hair, toned muscles, a small dress size, blindingly-white teeth, etc., really aren't that important compared to, say, world peace or global warming. But celebrities have to worry about every mouthful of food they eat and every new wrinkle. Imagine if all that energy were channeled toward something really significant, like helping the homeless or protecting the environment.

Rising Stars There's always another Hollywood "It" girl or fresh-faced model on the rise, which makes it hard to stay hot. And many models, stars, and "It" girls drop out of school at a young age, which means they don't have a high school or college diploma to fall back on when movie studios and modeling agencies don't come knocking anymore.

Missing Out on Normal Life Homecoming weekend, prom, lazy summer days with friends, family vacations, shopping trips to the mall—these things aren't hokey, they're real life. And stars often miss them because they're on set or traveling or just have a hard time getting back into the swing of things when they are home. True, they go to the Oscars every year, but that show is freakin' long and boring.

Making Money Off Girls' Dreams

Bogus modeling agencies and talent searches often charge steep up-front fees of nearly $1,000, plus an additional monthly fee, to post photos on a Web site. Agencies often also charge hundreds of dollars more for photographers, clothes, makeup, and modeling conventions—all with no guarantee of work or future earnings. Unfortunately, as long as models and stars are worshiped as role models, there will probably be girls starstruck enough to pay for a chance to get discovered.

Still not convinced? Just check out what stylists, managers, and modeling agents who work with celebrities every day say about stars' real lives.

"The competition is fierce because stars never know if their look is going to be 'in' the next day. Very few models eat whatever they want to without gaining weight. Most have their own personal trainers, [and some] girls become bulimic and take drugs to kill their appetites. They waste away to flesh and bone—and put pressure on themselves to be even skinnier." —Ursula, model booker and manager with Wilhelmina Models, Germany

"At publicity events and photo shoots, there's always tons of amazing free food, like a cookie bar and a pizza table. All the press agents, photographers, staff, and personal assistants get to indulge, but not the stars. They have to worry about looking good in a string bikini, but we can eat peanut butter cookies if we want."
—Madeleine, a publicist for top Hollywood celebrities

"Celebrities can't just go shopping at the mall or to the movies with friends. Plus they're in constant competition with someone newer, hotter, and more exciting threatening to steal their spotlight, which requires them to work hard every single day to maintain their image. Diets, trainers, voice coaches, appearances, the right clothes, the right boyfriend. All of it is calculated and rehearsed. I spend hours assuring the most beautiful men and women in the world that their butts don't look big in a particular pair of pants. What a waste of time!"
—Charlotte, Hollywood wardrobe stylist

"Lots of actresses have troubled relationships with food. Some obsess about how much they eat on a particular day and how they have to go to the gym twice as long to work it all off. Or they exist on just energy drinks and cigarettes. But the camera really does make you look ten pounds

heavier, so if they gain just a few pounds, it looks like a lot on screen. It's actually pretty easy not to get starstruck if you know what goes on behind the scenes. Who wants to constantly worry about dieting, exercise, grooming, etc. ?"—Stella, Hollywood wardrobe stylist

No wonder those disadvantages of stardom are kept so hush-hush. They'd ruin the mystique that keeps us starstruck.

Hype Free!

Not everyone agrees that models and stars are the best role models or should be the faces of success and beauty. In fact, lots of girls think they should be anything but.

"Just because stars are on TV and the radio doesn't mean they are special people. It's wrong that we look up to pretty women just because they can act or sing."
—*Samantha, 13*

"It's not fair that celebrities and stars get free clothes when they already have enough money to buy them." —*Gemma, 14*

"Every- one goes over the top for celebrities, but we should care about other people, like gymnasts and swimmers, not just swimsuit models." —*Faye, 13*

"Our culture is obsessed with women who do nothing for a living and become famous for it."
—*Shari, 16*

"How is looking pretty and showing off your body parts an accomplishment? Most of us are too preoccupied with Britney to learn about the amazing women of the world." —Rae, 15

"We're all human beings. Teachers, professors, and doctors should be as appreciated as stars because teachers help build bridges to kids' futures and doctors help keep us alive." —Tessa, 17

"Our culture is totally starstruck. Everyone has a favorite actress or singer that they worship, but no one talks about Rosa Parks or anyone else who has changed our country for the better." —Nicole, 13

In so many (too many!) parts of the world, women who *look* good are more recognizable than women who *do* good. In fact, since models became celebrities in the middle of the twentieth century, they've dictated the definitions of female beauty and success. Today other celebs, "It" girls, and pop stars share their mega fame and their influence. Together, they are the women most celebrated by the media, while so many others are virtually forgotten about or left on the sidelines because of *who* and *what* pays for most media aimed at young women. It's totally backward and needs to be changed.

Model Mania

"You meet interesting people and make a bundle of money."
—Tatiana Patitz, who's modeled for Vogue, Elle, and Calvin Klein

"We don't wake up for less than $10,000 a day."
—supermodel Linda Evangelista

"Let's be serious . . . My sister is an oncologist who went to school for fourteen years, and her income does not compete with mine."
—Veronica Webb, former Revlon spokesmodel

With all the fame and fortune showered on models, no wonder it seems like just about the best job around.

BACK TALK BLOG

☆ Models, stars, and other female celebrities are *the* most recognizable women in the world. Do they deserve their fame and fortune, or are there other women you think should be showered with praise and rewards?

☆ Do you feel pressured to look and be like the women you see in the media?

☆ Speak up on the blog.

chapter three

The Media

The media are everywhere, and they bombard you with images and information—from slick fashion magazines and best-selling books to fast-paced blockbuster movies, juicy reality TV shows, and racy music videos. From the latest CDs, radio shows, and MP3 downloads to text messages, the media shape our view of the world—and they play a big role in defining *who* and *what* is considered beautiful.

Even billboards on the side of the road, cars and buses "wrapped" in company logos, miniscreens playing commercials in office building elevators, telemarketing phone calls, slogans on baggage claim conveyor belts at the airport are all different forms of media, and they're *everywhere*. Just think about how much TV you watch on an average day, how many posters on the side of a telephone booth you pass, how much time you spend surfing the Web most nights, and the magazines you flip through with friends over lunch at school. It all adds up to a lot of media exposure.

Startling Stats

☆ Average time per week that Americans aged 2 to 17 spend watching television: 19 hours, 40 minutes

☆ Time per day that TV is on in an average U.S. home: 7 hours, 40 minutes

☆ Number of commercials seen by an average child in one year: 40,000

☆ Hours per year the average American child watches television: 1,023

☆ Hours per week average teen spends surfing the Internet, chatting, and writing e-mail: 16.5.

☆ Percentage of teens going online every day: more than 50 percent.

☆ $24 billion: the profits the video game industry, which is growing faster than any other entertainment market, earned worldwide in 2003.

WHOA! That's a lot of media exposure. It's everywhere, every day, all the time—that's what makes it so powerful. In fact, there are so many media messages swirling around all the time, it can be hard to separate them from reality. That's why it's important to know about how the media operate.

How the Media Do What They Do

Picture this: You're feeling good about your body and the way you look, and then you come across an ad for a shampoo that promises impossibly shiny hair or a toothpaste that makes teeth *really* white. Or you read in a magazine that your favorite star never leaves the house without a specific type of lip balm. Suddenly, you're feeling like your *real* body isn't good enough. Well know this: The media (on behalf of the companies that hire them) aim to plant the idea in our minds that we have a problem, and then offer us a product that will "fix" it—for a price, of course. They use cutting-edge technology to erase flaws like pimples or stretch marks or to improve models' appearances. Sometimes they even combine two or three photos, taking the head from one and the body from another in order to create a perfect image. And the media use all sorts of tricks and technology to make the sale:

Information Overload The human brain can only process about 8 frames of a movie or video

per second, yet there are 30 frames per second in most TV shows, and 24 frames per second in movies. That means images and messages appear and disappear before we even have a chance to make sense of them.

Product Placement When a character on a TV show says she'd die for a certain brand of soda, works with a name-brand computer, or drives a specific make of car, that's actually a hidden form of advertising that manufacturers pay for because it gets their product seen without the audience realizing it's watching advertising. Sneaky, eh? Because we're much less likely to walk out of a hot new movie or turn off our favorite TV shows than to flip past a magazine ad or change the channel during a commercial, this is a really valuable kind of advertising—and there will be much more of it in the future.

Hey! How'd That Get in Here?

*I*n the Disney film *Herbie: Fully Loaded,* Lindsay Lohan's character, Maggie Peyton, talks about craving Tropicana orange juice (instead of a generic juice) and lands a job at ESPN (instead of a no-name network). Are these specific preferences and details important to the story? Nope. Just product placement.

Creating Insecurities and Desire In order to sell products, the media and manufacturers make up problems, then offer a solution. Their ads and commercials imply that something is wrong with our bodies (like chronic bad breath, for instance) and then sell us a cure (the newest, best, most amazing mouthwash ever!). Or they create a fantasy world, like in a clothing catalog, where everything is so perfect, you're persuaded to buy their clothes just to try to capture a smidge of the idealized atmosphere in your own life.

"Buzz" and "Stealth" Marketing Some companies hire gorgeous models, trendy teens—even trustworthy adults like coaches and clergy—to talk up their products in public places. The actors pretend they're just normal, average people having a conversation that "happens" to be about a recently opened restaurant or a hip motor scooter to help get the name out there. Similarly, some publicists leak juicy information about their star clients so that everyone's buzzing about them at the same time they have a movie or CD being released.

Market Research Media and manufacturers also spend thousands of dollars on figuring out what their customers want. They host online chats, where young people are more apt to talk openly

about personal matters, hire teens to test out their products while they watch from behind a two-way mirror, and visit with kids and teens in their bedrooms and bathrooms to film them during their morning routines, then sell information about their habits to manufacturers. Scary. Worse still, they secretly videotape kids in toy stores to see what revs them up, and they make deals with schools to observe students in classrooms and even help design homework assignments that

The ABCs of Selling Stuff to Kids

Advertisers spend $15 billion—that's double the amount spent ten years ago—on marketing to kids. The scary thing is that it works: Infants recognize characters, colors, and symbols. And toddlers often ask for products by name. At six, kids can name more than two hundred brands. And 62 percent of twelve- and thirteen-year-olds report that buying certain products makes them feel better about themselves.

mention their product's name. To be fair, all this interaction also lets *us* influence *them*. However, since media and the manufacturers they work for often exploit the information in order to boost their sales, they have the upper hand.

Digital Enhancement Media images are perfected using advanced computer techniques that do everything, including slim down a model's thighs, erase her blemishes, enhance her cleavage, and add volume to her limp hair. Some magazines have even been caught manufacturing impossibly perfect images by pasting the head from one photo of a star to the body of another. No wonder they don't look like most real women and girls.

Turning a Blind Eye The media can choose to ignore a story or focus on a particular theme. They can promote opinions or products they like, while avoiding those they don't. They control what makes it onto the airwaves and into print and cyberspace. Also, many media outlets are owned by the same "parent" companies, which buy up music video stations, news organizations, book publishers, outdoor billboard associations, and radio networks. That means headquarters could decide to splash ads for the newest band to hit the radio all over its billboards at the same time that its television news stations run a clip about the band's sold out concert, while its cable channel keeps replaying the band's latest music video and the book publishing company launches a biography of the cute band members. In fact, companies feature cross-media campaigns all the time.

Making Changes

Understanding how the media operate is the first step to seeing through celebrity hype because it reveals what's real and what's made up. It also empowers you to take the best from the media (whatever's fun and cool) and leave the rest. So the next time you flip through your favorite magazine or watch a movie, use these questions to help get at the full picture:

1. *What's the point?* Is the ad/TV show/song/article/ movie/Web site/video game trying to sell something? Is it part of a buzz marketing campaign that's prepping you for the release of a new product?

2. *How does it work?* Does it project way more information than your brain can easily process or contain impossibly perfect images? Does it suggest you've got a problem, then offer a product as a solution?

3. *What's your gut reaction?* How does the media example make you feel about your body and lifestyle? Does it build your confidence, or make you feel like you have to improve yourself in some way? Does it offer a product that claims it can help you?

4. *What does it value?* Does it make it seem more important for girls to be sexy than smart? Does it show women with different body types and looks? What kind of woman or girl does it glorify?

5. *Who made it?* Can you figure out whether a large, wealthy corporation made it or a small, independent one? If it's a big company, can you determine what else it owns and identify any links to its other media outlets?

And follow these suggestions for making changes to the media that's already out there:

Be Aware

Form an opinion about what you like and don't in the media, like the portrayal of women and girls, by keeping up with new TV shows, Web sites and magazines, etc. Even if you don't respect a media example, check it out so that you can voice your opinion in an informed way.

Smoke and Mirrors

ots of top fashion photographers and celebrities who pose for cover shoots for big magazines like *Vogue* and *Vanity Fair* insist that their photos be perfected by Pascal Dangin, a New York–based photo retoucher who has improved cover images for such magazines as *W, Harper's Bazaar, Allure* and ads for Cover Girl cosmetics and *The Sopranos*. For $500 he can fix up a page inside the magazine, and for $20,000 he'll create a flawless cover image—no matter what the original looked like.

Speak Out

Don't like what you see? Then write to Web masters, magazine editors, manufacturers, advertisers, movie studios, and book publishers that create products with which you don't agree. Really want to make changes? Then make your own media! Find out if there are public-access TV or radio stations in your community and pitch a show that covers issues *you* think are important.

Support Media That Make a Difference

When you come across an empowering Web site, an alternative magazine, a great movie with an inspiring heroine, or a song with lyrics that mean something, send an e-mail blast to your friends or write an editorial for your school or local newspaper. Have your own Web page? Exchange links with sites you respect. And get to know independent ("indie") media sources, which can print whatever they want because they aren't pressured by the values and restrictions of a parent company.

Take a Break
Most entertainment today focuses around buying or paying for something (tickets to a concert, a DVD rental, shopping with friends). Try planning an activity that is free and has nothing to do with the media. Organize a huge group hike with all your friends or find volunteer work that you can do together, like face painting at a carnival for kids at the local shelter or hospital. Check the local paper for poetry slams or free lectures hosted by the women's center at a nearby university.

Behind the Scenes at Magazines

Magazines include a lot of great information. Most assign well-researched articles on hot topics to really great writers who get the full story. But as cool as mags are, it's important to know that since they make most of their money from advertisers buying up the pages in between the articles, they have limitations. For instance, a teen magazine probably wouldn't print an article about how girls are more beautiful *without* makeup, since the magazine depends on ads from big cosmetic companies to survive, and those companies aren't likely to advertise in an environment that's "hostile" to their products. But think of it this way: If the magazines didn't have ads, there would be no money to produce them. So in some ways, the compromise is worth it. Also, magazine editors can't always print everything they want to because sometimes they have to follow rules set by their parent companies. If the bosses decide they don't want to include a controversial topic—even if it's important to the readers and editors—it can get axed. Just like that. But the more input readers give to their favorite magazines about which topics interest them, the more likely a magazine will be to cover them.

Beyond the Media

The media are powerful, but they aren't alone in shaping definitions of beauty and success. Family, cultural traditions, boys, and friends can play a big part, too. Older women are under more pressure than ever before to deny the effects of aging, which can cause them to be hyperaware of their bodies *and* pass on that pressure to younger women unintentionally. Hanging out with friends who stress over every calorie can make it seem normal to mind every mouthful. (It's not.) And wanting attention from guys who are taught to worship models, stars, and "It" girls (more on that in chapter 5) can make things even worse. Ultimately *you* have to decide for yourself what makes a woman beautiful and successful, no matter what the media—or anyone else—tell you.

Share What You Know

Pass on what you know about how the media operate to help raise awareness and motivate others to make changes, too. And check out chapter 7 for even more ideas.

Hype Free!

Some girls are fed up with the media's made-up tricks and tactics and refuse to let them influence how they feel about themselves and which role models they choose. Check out these inspiring quotes:

"Magazines and ads basically say thin is in and everything else is not. Those words aren't *actually* printed in the magazine, but the pictures, articles, diet and fitness tips tell you what you should look like because they don't show any other options." —*Jessica, 17*

"The media have affected me negatively because every time I see such beautiful people on television, I think I look bad or have to try to look as good as them." —*Kerstin, 16*

"My friends all dress by what the media tell them looks good, even if it doesn't suit them. Sometimes even I dress how the media tells me to. All the girls I know, including myself, try to have the right body shape—the shape we see in the media." —*Hannah, 15*

"I don't think a girl should need a famous role model. I admire and look up to people I know and respect, which is much better than wanting to copy the lifestyle of a celebrity." —*Michelle, 17*

"I used to compare myself to media ideals, but now I refuse. It's such a waste of money and time! I wasted years of my life wanting to be something different, something I will never be." —*Jenny, 14*

The media aren't entirely bad. Magazines, TV shows, Web sites, etc., all contain valuable information and are also hip, entertaining, and fun. But they have an agenda, which is to sell products. And as you'll see in the next chapter, the sad truth about why the definition of beauty is so narrow—and the reason that some women are more celebrated by the media than others— is because expanding that definition would make the media and manufacturers less profitable.

BACK TALK BLOG

☆ Do you think what you see in the media is realistic?
☆ Do they feature the types of girls and women you consider role models?
☆ Do media images make you feel empowered and confident, or unsure of yourself, your abilities, and your appearance?
☆ What do you think is missing from media images?
☆ Rant and rave on the blog!

chapter four

The Look

Different eras and cultures have always had their own ideas of female beauty. For centuries, the Chinese bound young girls' feet to keep them dainty even though it made basic activities—like, um, walking—nearly impossible. And during the eighteenth and nineteenth centuries in Europe and America, ultra slim waists were *the* thing to have, so women wore tight corsets that sometimes led to fainting and malformation of the abdomen. In many countries outside Europe and North America, plumpness is sexy and larger women are celebrated. Brides in central Africa are sent to fattening farms several weeks before their weddings, and in Latino communities, *beautiful* usually means curvy figures with round hips and shapely breasts. In India, having a little extra padding around the midriff is beautiful because it means being wealthy enough to avoid hard work that builds muscle. Today, unnatural thinness and perfection are all the rage, leading many women and girls to crash-diet, surgically alter their bodies, and abuse exercise. So then where does this unhealthy and unnatural definition of beauty come from?

The Definition du Jour

Thinness, good hair, toned muscles, a hairless body, a polished image, white teeth, and clear skin—today's look does *not* celebrate the body in its natural state. It requires expensive beauty treatments and products like

exfoliation, electrolysis, facials, liposuction, high-lights, spray tans, tooth bleaching, manicures, gym memberships, botox injections, designer cosmetics and

Why Skin is In

Belly-baring tank tops, super-low-cut jeans, ultrashort miniskirts—all those fashions show off the body parts important to today's definition of beauty, like a flat stomach or long legs. When you see scantily clad starlets and models on the red carpet or even a girl at school showing lots of skin, it's like they're saying, "I've got 'the look'! I'm as skinny and pretty as women celebrated for being beautiful!" They've figured out that "the look" is a key to perks and praise, so they're trying to prove they've got what it takes.

skincare lines, trendy clothing, jewelry loans from posh boutiques, and plastic surgery and experts such as wardrobe stylists, dermatologists, personal trainers, and nutrition coaches. There's nothing honest, easy, or genuine about "the look." It's a completely made up, high-maintenance, costly definition of beauty that's nearly impossible to obtain—even for models, actresses, and stars. In fact, supermodel Cindy Crawford reportedly once said that even *she* wishes she woke up looking like Cindy Crawford. And sexy actresses like Julia Roberts, Kim Basinger, and Madonna have all hired body doubles (actresses with bodies that are considered as close to perfection as possible) to stand in for them on revealing movie scenes.

But if this look is so hard to achieve, why does it define beautiful? Well, as explained in chapter 3, the media have a financial interest in keeping us as starstruck as possible so that we buy the products made by them and other manufacturers. This is especially true when it comes to the beauty, fashion, and diet–weight loss industries, which make thousands of products and spend millions on advertising them. To convince us that "the look" *is* beautiful, the media and advertisers start by acting like it is. Until a star or model is clinically diagnosed with an eating disorder and goes public about her struggle, the media rarely call her too thin—even though recent winners of the Miss America pageants have had body mass indexes or BMI, a measurement of the relative percentages of fat and muscle mass in the body) considered "malnourished" by current standards of the World Health Organization. Instead, they praise ultrathin figures and hype diets that make them possible, which sends a clear

and distressing message: get "the look" and get re-
warded.

Unfortunately, "the look" is spreading. As western
companies increasingly export their products to de-
velop new markets, and girls and women see (via the
media) the rewards "beautiful" women get, beauty
standards are changing worldwide. Girls in Nigeria are
reportedly trying to lose weight in order to be as thin
as six-foot-tall Agbani Darego, the first African win-
ner of the Miss World beauty competition since its
launch in 1951. Until 2002, local African judges had
entered contestants that symbolized the African ideal
of beauty: voluptuous with ample backsides and
breasts. However, it was Darego, with her tall frame

and skinny body, who earned the honor of being considered one of the most beautiful women in the world, which is ironic, since she isn't considered particularly attractive by most Nigerians. And when TV was introduced to the Pacific island nation of Fiji in 1995, programs that celebrate "the look"—like '90s nighttime soaps *Melrose Place* and *Beverly Hills, 90210*—caused 74 percent of Fijian girls to feel "too big or fat" within three years.

Buying the Look

The world spends $38 billion on hair-care products, $24 billion on skin care, $18 billion on makeup, and $15 billion on perfumes every year. Scary. Just like the prices for top-quality beauty services:

☆ A haircut with Sally Hershberger, the bi-coastal stylist who counts Meg Ryan, Renée Zellweger, and Nicole Kidman among her clients: $600

☆ A custom-designed facial at Ole Henriksen, the Hollywood skin care salon that boasts clients like Charlize Theron, Julia Stiles, and Alanis Morissette: $105

☆ A manicure and pedicure at J. Sisters International, a New York spa favored by Gwyneth Paltrow and models Naomi Campbell and Christy Turlington: $100

☆ A seaweed body wrap at New York's Mario Badescu skin care salon, which is frequented by Liv Tyler, Mischa Barton, Kate Moss, and Hilary Swank: $105

Where does that leave women and girls who can't afford to pay? Priced out of being pretty?

Since some people are willing to pay big bucks for "the look," plastic surgery is exploding. Between 1997 and 2003, the number of cosmetic procedures increased in America by over 220 percent, and teens are increasingly being given breast augmentations as graduation gifts. In one year, the number of girls eighteen and younger getting breast implants jumped nearly threefold, from 3,872 in 2002 to 11,326 in 2003.

One New York plastic surgeon even hosts hip plastic surgery informational evenings at cool nightclubs, where cutting-edge computer technology shows girls how their appearance could be "improved" by a little nip and tuck, while another surgeon in Miami is nick-named "Dr. Boobner" because he performs an average of five implant surgeries a day.

Of course, plastic surgery also helps with scars after serious accidents or reconstruction after illness. But even the American Society of Plastic Surgeons thinks extreme makeover television shows and celebrity look-alike contests contribute to the rise in plastic surgery by making it seem normal to buy artificial enhancements as a way to copy media ideals and be happy.

Paying the Price

The problem with "the look" is that it requires an all-out war on our bodies. Every stray hair, wrinkle, pound of extra flesh, freckle, blemish, stain, etc., is an intolerable imperfection dealt with by painful, time-consuming, and expensive procedures. Monitoring what's "wrong" with our bodies and agonizing over "flaws" is exhausting, expensive, time-consuming, and downright boring. Not to mention that all that energy could be spent on far more important endeavors. And since "the look" doesn't much resemble what girls and women look like naturally, it messes up what we—and as you'll see in chapter 5, guys—think of as pretty. In fact, 59 percent of teen girls are reportedly dissatisfied with their body shape, 66 percent desire to lose weight, and over half report that the appearance of models in

Money to Burn (Plus Vacuum and Inject, Too)

Before hooking up with Ashton Kutcher, actress Demi Moore reportedly had a $400,000 total-body makeover:

- ☆ Botox injections in her face at a cost of $4,000 three times per year
- ☆ Surgery costing $10,000 to replace her breast implants with smaller ones
- ☆ Liposuction worth $15,000 to suck fat out of her stomach, buttocks, and thighs
- ☆ Collagen injections in her lips and other skin treatments that cost $6,240
- ☆ White porcelain veneers for her teeth that cost $16,000
- ☆ A nutritionist that cost $22,000
- ☆ A personal trainer for $25,000
- ☆ A $15,600 yoga instructor
- ☆ A kickboxing coach for $230,000

With that kind of cash and expert assistance, who wouldn't look amazing?

the magazines influences their image of a perfect female body. And some girls are more afraid of becoming fat than they are of nuclear war, cancer, or losing their parents. Just listen to these girls:

"I spend thousands on facials, manicures, pedicures, hair treatments, makeup, beauty products, clothes, and I carry a mirror everywhere I go. I never make friends with anyone prettier or sexier than me."
—Angelique, 14

"My four friends don't eat lunch because they want to lose weight, yet they're already so small, there's no weight to lose!"
—Nicole, 15

"I was twelve when I first started comparing myself to models. I would wake up feeling happy with myself and my body, but then one magazine cover could dash it all. When I was sixteen, I was diagnosed with anorexia and dropped a ton of weight. I was really sick, but yet the skinnier I became, the more attention and compliments I got."
—*Heather, 19*

"Somedays, I don't eat dinner so my stomach will lose fat. I used to wear comfortable baggy clothes like T-shirts and sweats. Now I wear tight pants, a tight skirt, high shoes, and makeup. I want to be like J. Lo and all those other famous women." —*Jasmine, 13*

"An extremely small amount of women in the world have the model look, and there are thousands of us trying to copy them. Instead of boosting our self-esteem it causes us to hurt ourselves at a time when we should be growing and finding out what we like about ourselves."
—*Abby, 16*

"I'm guilty of not liking my body at all and I hate feeling this way. I have been eating healthier trying to lose weight because I want to just be skinny. All of my friends say I look fine, but I won't listen to them. I want people to look at me and think I am just as pretty as the next girl." —*Kerri, 15*

"I'm African American, and I have the type of body they sing about in rap videos: a 36DDD chest and a round 'ghetto booty.' There are no positive images in the media of girls who look like me. It makes me feel like I'm not pretty and that my body type isn't considered desirable. Aren't I beautiful, too?" —*Jessica, 17*

"I feel fat. I know I'm not, but all the stuff I see in the media makes me feel that way." —*Diana, 17*

Bread Is Not the Enemy

Rachel Elizabeth Huskey, sixteen, from Sturgeon, Missouri, died from heart failure after following a low-carbohydrate diet, which allowed plenty of fatty cheeses and meats but restricted breads, cereals, and fruits and vegetables because they are mistakenly believed to cause weight gain. The media constantly report on stars who follow similar diets but often forget to mention that the doctor who pioneered low-carb living as a surefire way to lose weight apparently died from heart disease, too.

Fight Back

No matter what the limited media images suggest, there are lots of ways to be beautiful. Beauty isn't about buying products to achieve a certain look or copying styles modeled by celebrities in ads or on magazine covers. It's about looking and feeling good in your own skin. Do that by being you, and checking out these tips:

Refuse to Obsess About Your Weight Who got to decide what the ideal weight for a pretty woman should be? More important, why should we try to live up to someone else's definition? Weight is really nothing more than numbers on a scale. Forget about them, and concentrate on being healthy and comfortable with your body.

Stop Comparing Remember that media images are digitally enhanced, and models, stars, and "It" girls spend oodles of time and money to look like they do. Enjoy wearing makeup and the latest fashions, just don't worry about replicating "the look" in your real life.

Love Your Parts Stop wishing you had hair like one model and a flat stomach like another. You're a whole package, and every part is exactly as it's supposed to be, whether or not it compares to "the look."

The Skinny on Fat

Ironically, thinness has become the symbol of beauty at a time when nearly one third of American adults over the age of twenty (over 60 million people) are obese, and among children six to nineteen, 16 percent (over 9 million young people) are considered overweight. Yet while many indulge in high-calorie processed foods, enormous portions, and sedentary pastimes like IMing, about 8 million Americans suffer from eating disorders and approximately 90 percent of them are young women. These illnesses are on the rise worldwide, and the average age of sufferers is dropping rapidly, with problems showing up in girls as young as nine. There's no simple explanation for anorexia, bulimia, exercise abuse, and orthorexia (an obsession with healthy food and lifestyle), but psychological factors like temperament, family history, and social pressure can all play a part. Get more information and help for these disorders in the Resources section at the back of this book.

Don't Believe the Hype Stars and models always say they stay skinny thanks to high metabolisms. Sh-yeah, right. Even if it were true, every body is different. So respect yours for its uniqueness instead of punishing it for not being like someone else's.

Take the Best, Leave the Rest The media send mixed messages by featuring positive articles, characters, and photos of real women juxtaposed with diet tips and thin role models. Have fun with the good stuff, and ignore the junk.

Value Strength and Skills—Not Thinness The media put a lot of emphasis on exercising to look good and get skinny. Booooo. Exercise to have

fun, get healthy, learn new skills, and make friends who have similar interests.

Hype Free!

The truth is lots of girls *hate* trying to live up to "the look." They don't hate the idea of beauty or pretty things, just the feeling that they'll never look as good as the women considered beautiful—and the implication that they're less desirable, lovable, and valuable than those who are.

"Fashion, beauty, and what's in are always changing. I'm happy with my body because I'm unique, as cheesy as that sounds, and I like all the things my body can do, and I don't want to change that."
—*Anna, 14*

"I feel best about myself when I do something I thought I couldn't do, like get a top grade in math or run a whole mile in 9 minutes and 44 seconds. I can achieve things other people can't, and I can do things body-obsessed stars can't do."
—*Kimberly, 14*

"I want to change today's beauty standards to show that you don't have to have a model look to be beautiful, and you also don't have to be rich or famous. There should be more emphasis on personality, personal goals, and dreams than on a great body." —*Jennifer, 16*

"I would bring back curves! No more razor burns and bikini waxes! High-fashion clothing would come in all sizes, and big women would be celebrated!"
—*Dana, 16*

"Celebrities wear practically nothing these days. I wish they seemed more natural and normal—and that we didn't feel like we needed to dye our hair or get fake tans."
—*Hannah, 15*

"I'm so sick of stars and models and their emaciated bodies, plus poses that make them look really vulnerable and childlike instead of strong and proud." —*Emily, 17*

Everyone wants to be considered pretty—to be envied and praised and copied. In fact, it's hard *not* to want it given the rewards and special treatment showered on those who are. But here's the truth: It's not our bodies that need changing or that need to look more like what's pictured most frequently in the media. It's made-up unrealistic beauty standards—promoted by companies that want to sell us products—that need to change to look more like us.

 BACK TALK BLOG

☆ What do *you* consider beautiful?
☆ Are you under pressure to live up to current beauty ideals?
☆ If so, from whom—yourself?
☆ The media? Boys?
☆ How do you think beauty and success should be defined?
☆ What do you think can be done to help make these changes happen?
☆ Blog your thoughts and ideas.

chapter five

Boys

Chances are you've heard guys make comments about celebrities like "Dude, she's so hot!" or "I'm gonna marry someone just like that." Or maybe you know some boys who act like stars and models are their idea of the perfect girl. Well, boys aren't born thinking that celebrities are more valuable or desirable than other women, they learn it.

Boys Don't Cry

It must be really hard to be a guy. From an early age,

they're bombarded with messages from the media—and even family and friends—about what is "manly" and cool. In order to escape being considered geeks or losers, they're pressured to follow strict rules such as:

☆ Don't cry
☆ Don't be a wuss
☆ Hang tough
☆ Keep a stiff upper lip
☆ Don't act like a girl or a "fag"
☆ Be cool
☆ Get the girl
☆ Go for it!
☆ Be a leader
☆ Be confident
☆ Be one of the guys
☆ Be good at sports

Since guys aren't supposed to talk openly about their fears or emotions, some end up keeping their feelings

Boys and Their Toys

Guys watch more TV than girls (81 percent vs. 75 percent) and are more than twice as likely as girls to play video games (40 percent vs. 18 percent) or use the Internet (15 percent vs. 10 percent), which means they are subjected to a *lot* of media messages.

bottled up until they explode into anger. They're also taught to control and dominate situations and that real

"Dude, Do I Look Fat in This?"

Throughout history, guys have generally been wash 'n' go, spending less time fussing over appearance than girls. But that's changing as images of male performers and athletes baring their toned, lean bodies are increasingly featured on billboards and magazine covers. Men's shopping magazines, makeover reality shows, and spas with treatments just for guys are encouraging guys to spend time on looking good and causing boys to feel pressure about their looks. Twenty years ago, experts estimated that for every ten to fifteen women with anorexia or bulimia, there was one man. Today the ratio is more like for every three female cases, there's one male case. And out of the more than 7.4 million plastic surgery procedures performed in the United States in 2003, 14 percent were on men, which was up 14 percent over the year before. Studies also show that when ten-year-old girls and boys watched a music video by Britney Spears or a clip from the TV show *Friends*, both the boys and the girls reported feeling dissatisfied with their bodies.

men don't do housework or cooking (unless it's to get laughs or because they happen to be celebrity chefs). Most important, they're generally encouraged to think that their accomplishments are more important than their appearance.

No-Good, Dirty, Rotten Media Messages . . .

The media play a big role in influencing guys to think that models and stars—or others who have "the look"— are the most desirable and valuable girls around. They also suggest that guys deserve such superior women— and make it seem like it's easy to get with one, which is the hook used to keep guys buying. Just check out how these actual examples feed the fantasy.

☆ In May 2000, Simon & Schuster Interactive released a video game called *Panty Raider: From Here to Immaturity*. The game is based on the idea that male aliens become obsessed with super gorgeous human models, who are held up as the highest and most desirable ideal of female beauty. To win the game, players must strip the supermodels down to their underwear then provide photographs of them to the aliens, who threaten to destroy Earth if they don't get to keep looking at the superior women. Both the aliens and the male players understand that looking at naked supermodels is worth anything—even the risk of intergalactic disaster.

☆ This advice column Q & A appeared on a Web site for guys called *www.girlsandsports.com*. The message that stars and models are more desirable and valuable than other women couldn't be any clearer.

Dear Bradley,
I met a really hot "model" but she is equally annoying. It

would be good to be seen in public with her, but I think I might hate her. Any advice? —Matt, La Jolla, CA

Dear Matt,

Please do not e-mail me to tell me you're not going to date a model because you think she's annoying. I don't care if you hate her. She's a model!!

Stop making a rookie mistake and overrating personality. No girl you ever meet will be as fun to talk to or hang out with as one of your guy friends. In the long list of requirements we look for in girls, personality ranks fifteenth or sixteenth; right above her cooking skills and right below her ability to quietly entertain herself while you're watching a football game.

In fact, aspects of a girl's physical appearance, including her body, face, legs, breasts, etc., dominate the top 10 list of traits that are most important to us. If the girl had a personality (just like if she had a goldfish), that would be nice, but DO NOT make it a prerequisite for dating her. Just remember, you don't sleep with a personality. —Bradley

☆ Since 1964, *Sports Illustrated*—which is read by 23 million adults each week, including over 18 million men—has been putting out its Swimsuit Issue during the winter sports lull between the Super Bowl and the start of the summer baseball season. Over the years, the magazine has featured many scantily clad models on its Swimsuit Issue covers and in its pages, but it wasn't until 1987 that a female athlete, track-and-field Olympian Jackie Joyner-Kersee, was actually featured on the cover of a regular issue, implying that models who look good in bathing suits deserve to be cover girls of a sports magazine more than talented female athletes.

☆ In Los Angeles, California, a company called Model Quality Introductions runs a dating service for "high caliber men, who are attractive, affluent, fun, polished, intelligent, and looking for a committed relationship." The selling point: All of the women that clients are set up with are of "model quality." In other words, the company makes it seem that the best men are wealthy and successful at business, and the best women are models—or those who look like them.

Nothing subtle about those media messages, eh? They pretty clearly suggest that when it comes to girls and women, models, stars, and celebrities—and those who look like them—are the crème de la crème, da bomb, the elite, first class, top choice. They also imply not only that guys deserve the best, but that it's within their reach. And since guys don't have as many cool alternative media sources or role models as girls do (check out chapter 6 and the resources at the end of the book), many boys grow up believing them.

. . . And Their Effect

The media messages that reach boys have a clear influence on the way that some of them think about girls and beauty. Just check out these comments from real guys:

"I would definitely like to date a model so I could show her off to everybody whenever we were out together." —*José, 18*

"The best part about dating a model or star would be being famous, too. How cool would it be to share some of the spotlight?!" —*Zachary, 15*

"Haven't all guys dreamed of dating models and stars? We all see fame and beauty and want to be like that. There would be so many perks to dating a famous person, it's not even funny." —*Robert, 15*

"Dating someone famous would mean being seen on TV and in tabloids. I'd become the most popular guy at school." —*Chris, 15*

"If I had to choose between dating a model-star and the prettiest girl at my school, I'd choose the model. DEFINITELY!" —*Scott, 14*

"Yeah, I've dreamed of dating models or stars. If I had to choose between dating the girl next door and a model, I'd choose the model. Scoring with that kind of girl is a huge priority with me and my friends." —*T. J., 17*

"Don't ALL guys dream of dating a star?" —*Robert, 15*

The most annoying part about guys who've fallen for the hype is that they often think that girls who try to educate them are just jealous. But that just shows that guys aren't really being taught to know the difference between what's made up and what's real.

Sisterhood of the Offensive T-shirt

Paris Hilton was once spotted in Los Angeles wearing a pink baby tee that read, "Your Boyfriend Wants Me." Way to reinforce the bogus idea that girls who have "the look" or a label like "It girl" are more desirable than others, Paris. Thanks fer nothin'.

The Trickle Down Effect

Lots of girls are troubled by guys' attitudes because they like boys and want to be considered pretty and attractive by them. But they don't want to have to live up to guys' fantasies that result from all the celebrity hype. Just listen to how torn up some girls are:

"We all want a handsome, sweet husband to start a family and grow old with. But to start on the path to that dream, you need to get a guy, and to get a guy you need to look perfect."
—*Lindsey, 15*

"All girls want the greatest-looking guy. But the only way to get him is to be the most perfect-looking girl." —*Faye, 13*

"When I hear guys talking about how hot stars are, I keep quiet because I'm jealous that they aren't talking about me that way."
—*Lexi, 15*

"I wish we didn't feel like we have to dress sexy to get a guy or please guys. It's so immature and stupid. Guys would rather date a starlet so they can boast, 'Look who I have as a girlfriend!'" —*Jennifer, 16*

"When guys talk about other girls in front of me, it makes me feel like my body isn't good enough. I want to ask, 'What is it that makes her so hot?' If she were mean and snotty, would you still like her?' It's personality—not just looks and fame—that matter."
—Tessa, 17

"When I hear guys talking about a model or star, I get jealous and disgusted at the same time. I would love to be the girl that ALL the guys wanted to be with, but then I think about what they're saying about her and I don't want to anymore." —Lauren, 15

In fact, guys should be equally as troubled about these media messages because they not only make girls and women seem like nothing more than sex objects, they treat guys like simpleminded morons who care more about looks and labels than personality. And that's just plain wrong, because there are tons of guys out there who see through celebrity hype and know how to recognize real beauty.

Helping Those in Need

Guys need to see how the media overvalue stars, models, and celebrities in men's media and how that probably affects their ideas of beauty and attitudes toward girls. Unfortunately, that's not likely to happen on its own, so it's up to us to help educate them. Either that or continue living with their unrealistic expectations. Here are some tips for getting started:

Let Guys Off the Hook . . . a Little   Remember that guys worry a lot about fitting in and being like their friends. And while that's no excuse for insensitive behavior, they truly might not realize that by trying to be cool, they've bought into media messages that many girls find offensive.

Don't Ignore Their Comments   If it bothers you when guys talk about stars like they are more desirable and important than other girls and women, speak up. Brushing them off with a "boys will be boys" attitude signals that you think their behavior and remarks are acceptable.

Spread the Word   Remind guys that images of stars and celebrities are usually airbrushed and retouched, plus some stars battle eating disorders to keep thin. If they act like they don't care, point out that appearance standards for guys are getting tougher, and that soon there will be just as much pressure on them to conform to a certain look as there is for girls.

Reach Out Approach your guy friends one-on-one, when they're away from all their buddies, and explain why hearing them rave about stars and models makes you feel uncomfortable. If they laugh or say you're just jealous, walk away. It's not worth getting hassled over. But know that you might have given them something to think about.

Hype Free . . . Boys!

Luckily, not all boys buy into celebrity hype. Some realize that the definitions and ideals that the media play up are unrealistic. These heroes are interested in *real* girls, not just those who have the right look or label.

"Supermodels and actresses are so made up. Everything they do is for a public image or the companies they work for. Plus, it's unlikely they look like they do in all the photo shoots or movies when they wake up in the morning." —*Alecks, 14*

"It's not cool to date someone for their looks. It's about personality. Sometimes my friends and I talk about stars, but we wouldn't really want to go out with them. Besides, we know we don't have a chance with any of them, anyway!" —*Kane, 14*

"I've known for a long time that pictures of stars and models are airbrushed and fixed on computers, and I hate it! The celebrities are COMPLETELY fake." —*Wade, 14*

"I've dreamed of dating models and actresses maybe once or twice, but a real girl is ultimately more attractive to me because I can talk to her." —*Matt, 17*

"Me and my friends sit around and discuss which celebrities are hot and which celebrities aren't but I never dream of dating one. I like to stick to reality because unless I become a star, I won't be dating one." —*Troy, 16*

"I think all the media images raise our expectations of normal girls, and that makes them look down on themselves. But they shouldn't!" —*Thomas, 15*

Boys are as vulnerable to media messages as girls are—maybe even more so since there are fewer positive alternatives and unconventional role models out there. But if they're made aware of how limited and biased the representations of female beauty are in men's media, then there's hope that they'll join—or at least support us—in making changes.

BACK TALK BLOG

☆ Do you know guys who buy into the hype about stars and models? Does it make you feel less valuable or desirable than models, actresses, celebutantes, pop stars, and those who look like them?

☆ Do you have some of your own snappy comebacks that have worked in conversations to show guys that looks and labels don't define female beauty and desirability?

☆ Share your strategies on the blog.

chapter six

Real Role Models

What makes a good role model: a tiny dress size and shiny hair or inner qualities? Is it more important for role models to be runway ready or ready to stand up for what they believe in? And who deserves more recognition and praise: women who have all the help in the world to look good or women who help make the world a better place?

Outstanding role models—women who offer more to admire than a bikini body and a bright smile—make important contributions in business, politics, sports, social activism, and even fashion. Yet they are less visible because their images and work often don't help sell beauty products, movie tickets, diet plans, gossip magazines, trendy new clothes, etc. Meet some of them here, and find out what they think about celebrity hype and celebrating real beauty.

Meghan Boone, founder of Zeta Omega Eta, a feminist sorority

Meghan Boone, twenty-one, grew up wanting to be a model. She idolized her cousin who worked in the industry and noticed that models were considered way more beautiful and special than other girls. When she got to college, she discovered that lots of girls had noticed the same sorts of things—and were totally sick of it. So she and her best friend, Anne-Louise Marquis, founded Zeta Omega Eta, a feminist sorority with activist goals. Instead of throwing wild parties, the Zetas organize campuswide lectures on topics like the women's movement and volunteer with elderly women at a local nursing home. And by banding together, they're making a difference.

"My extended family always made a big deal over my cousin because of her modeling. She's tall, with perfect skin and big boobs—and it was always, 'Did you see her in the magazine?! Look at her new pictures!' I saw from an early age that because of her looks, people paid more attention to her. And it made me want the same thing for myself.

"When I was thirteen, I got portfolio photos and went to about six months of casting calls with no luck. My agent suggested I lose fifteen pounds and have my ears—which just happen to be large—pinned back. She also wanted me to have my skin resurfaced where I have a scar on my chest from heart surgery I had as a child. At first her suggestions made me feel really bad about myself, but then I thought, 'I *like* the fact that my ears stick out, and if I didn't have my scar I wouldn't be alive!" So I said no. Part of me still wanted to have everything my cousin did, but trying to be a model wasn't worth changing myself.

"At college, I hated the fact that fraternities and sororities discriminated on the basis of sex—and how a lot of the guys treated girls. So my friend and I decided we'd try to start a Greek organization that accepted both guys and girls. We didn't know if it would take off, but at the first meeting, forty-two people showed up when we expected only seven! Once we started talking, we realized that we *all* had problems with the situation for women on campus and today's beauty standards. Everyone felt like she was the only one who thought she wasn't pretty enough, or didn't know how to wear her hair, or couldn't make herself live on cucumbers alone. But we discovered so many of us were struggling with the same things—and Zeta is raising awareness about these issues and trying to make changes.

"I could probably stand to lose five pounds, but I am happy with my body—and being happy is much more important to me than being thin. Besides, being 'beautiful' isn't a defining quality. I wouldn't be proud of it when I'm eighty. And there are so many more constructive ways we can spend our time than obsessing over appearance."

Reality Star

Actress Kate Winslet, who's always been honest about being comfortable with her body naturally, claims the size of her thighs was once reduced by about a third for the cover of the British men's magazine GQ. She fought back by releasing a statement saying: "The retouching is excessive. I do not look like that and more importantly I don't desire to look like that." You tell 'em, Luv.

Brittany Clifford, founder of Fuzzy Feet

Brittany Clifford, sixteen, thinks there's nothing worse than being sick and not having comfy pajamas to lounge in or cozy slippers to shuffle around in. So since 2002, she's collected and given away over four thousand pairs of cuddly, cheery slippers to hospitalized children in Phoenix, Los Angeles, and New York City to make them a bit more comfortable while away from home. In 2003, Brittany was chosen as one of the top two youth volunteers in her home state of Arizona and was named a state honoree in the prestigious Prudential Spirit of Community Awards. In 2004, she won a "Brick Award" from Do Something, a nonprofit organization that encourages youth community involvement. That meant a $5,000 grant for Fuzzy Feet and another $5,000 grant for her education. Obviously for Brittany, making a difference is way more important than getting caught up in celebrity hype.

"When I was little, I thought it would be cool to be a star because of the lifestyle, the free clothes, and having people wait on you. Then when I was twelve, my friend Michael—who was born with a bad heart—was in the hospital for surgery. When I visited him, he complained that his feet were cold. A few days later, I passed a pair of crazy gorilla slippers in a store and I bought them for Michael right away! He started wearing them around the hospital and all the other kids kept asking him where he got them. They were envious of the cool slippers—and that Michael had gotten a gift. I wished I could buy slippers for all of them, but I

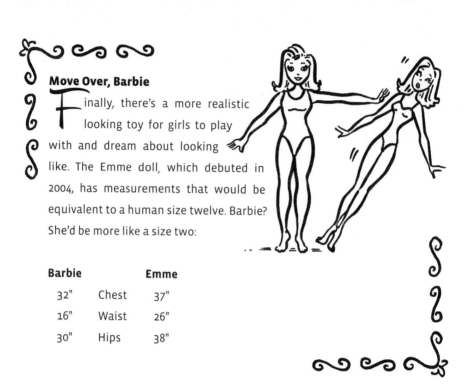

Move Over, Barbie

Finally, there's a more realistic looking toy for girls to play with and dream about looking like. The Emme doll, which debuted in 2004, has measurements that would be equivalent to a human size twelve. Barbie? She'd be more like a size two:

Barbie		Emme
32"	Chest	37"
16"	Waist	26"
30"	Hips	38"

knew my family would go broke if I did. So I decided to try to get them donated somehow.

"At the beginning, I thought we were just keeping kids from being cold, but now Fuzzy Feet has become a way to show sick children that someone cares and is thinking about them. Once, a boy came into the playroom where we were passing out slippers and chose a really big bumblebee pair. A little while later, the hospital director told me the boy's mother was crying, she was so touched, and that the boy went right from the playroom into heart surgery—and he asked to keep his slippers on during the operation.

"Some of my friends don't believe that working with kids can be more satisfying than being a star. I just invite them to come to the hospital and experience for themselves what it's like to help brighten the day of a child who really needs it. I just think the feeling of helping someone else and brightening someone else's day is better than dancing around with a flat midriff. It's way more rewarding to help others and make a difference."

Lisa Jervis and Andi Zeisler, founders of *Bitch* magazine, "The Feminist Response to Pop Culture"

Andi, thirty-three, and Lisa, thirty-three, *love* pop culture. Since graduating from college, they've been hashing out the good and the bad in magazines and

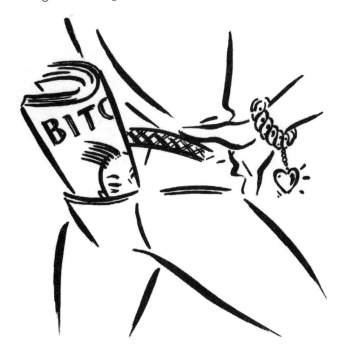

discussing what's right and wrong with their favorite TV shows. In 1996, they finally got so fed up with what the media was focusing on—and ignoring—when it comes to girls and women, they founded *Bitch*, a magazine in which these issues and more could be debated.

Why name the magazine *Bitch*? Because when the word is used as an insult, it's often directed at women who speak their minds and express their opinions. And they're out to show there's nothing wrong with that.

Lisa: "I was totally starstruck as a kid. I don't think I would have ended up where I am if I hadn't been affected by the images and ideals taught by the media. I didn't have terrible skin or anything like that, but it was so easy to start thinking 'Oh, I wish my hair were different. Maybe this ad is right! If I buy that product, maybe my hair will become perfectly smooth and I'll be so much happier.'

"It's almost impossible to grow up in our culture and not have some crazy body image issues, but I think if girls—make that everyone—learn to see how crazy these images are and the universal struggles against our bodies they can lead to, it can help us resist getting caught up in them.

People always say 'But it's *women* and *girls* who buy magazines (or go to see movies, etc.). If they didn't like them, they wouldn't spend their money.' My response is this: Just because a starving person will eat some dry toast doesn't mean she wouldn't rather have a roast beef sandwich. The market does not give us what we want. It actually gives us a choice within pretty narrow limitations of what manufacturers make available. It's not the case that if women were interested in more than fashion and hair and makeup that media for women would be different. The reality is that if media made for women and girls were *funded* differently, *then* their content would be different.

Andi and I wanted to do something active, effective, and public to try to make changes—that's why we founded

Bitch. A lot of people doubted us—and we doubted our-selves, too. We weren't really sure if others wanted to talk and read critiques about how women are portrayed in the media and other important issues that affect the lives of girls and women. But when the first issue hit the newsstands, there was a really strong response. It proved to us that we definitely aren't the only people who care about this stuff."

Andi: "When I was a girl, I was so unaware of mea-suring myself against media ideals. But I had a friend who was really obsessed with a model featured regularly in *Seventeen,* and I just couldn't understand why she looked up to a person that she didn't know anything about. She idolized her just because she had the look that got her into a popular magazine. I didn't get it.

"My mother worked in the beauty industry, so she was conscious of appearance and always made sure I looked good and had cute clothes. But I was also a tomboy into a ton of activities like soccer, softball, ice skating, art lessons, piano, baseball, and rocket club, where one of the female teachers in my school taught us to make rockets out of cardboard tubing and small

Wrinkles Rock

In 2004, Dove beauty products launched the Campaign for Real Beauty, an ad campaign using models that didn't have "the Look" (a teen covered with freckles, a flat-chested twentysomething, a happily ageing senior citizen) to raise questions about definitions of beauty. Critics accused Dove of exploiting women's dissatisfaction with their bodies to sell products. Maybe. But how refreshing to praise a smil-ing, wrinkled woman's face instead of claiming it needs improvement.

parachutes! I was constantly occupied and felt good about all the things I was learning, so I didn't base my worth or future dreams on appearance. But if I had media surrounding me all the time telling me what to do to be a certain way like girls do today, I might have turned out differently.

"When we started *Bitch*, Lisa and I definitely agreed that the media we liked, chiefly magazines and TV, didn't really address issues we thought were really important. We were mad that Kelly on *Beverly Hills, 90210* reverted to baby talk every time she was within earshot of a cute boy and couldn't understand why no journalists were commenting on stuff like that. The most important thing for us with *Bitch* is to redefine feminism and make people see that it's a broad subject that touches on so many aspects of all of our lives. We wanted to create something with an activist angle that people would *want* to read—not something that would make people feel like they were being told to eat all their broccoli. Judging from letters we get from readers who tell us that *Bitch* means a lot to them and has changed their lives, we're on the right track."

Swin Cash, forward on the WNBA's Detroit Shock

Swintayla Cash, twenty-five, is the type of person who lives by the motto "Go for it!" In high school she lettered in track in addition to being on the basketball team and president of the student council. On her college team, she was consistently voted Most Outstanding Player. And as professional, she scores an average of nine points per game and was member of the 2004 U.S. National Team that won a gold medal at the Olympics in Athens, Greece. But she's also into making a difference, which she does by funding a $1,000 scholarship, in her hometown of McKeesport, Pennsylvania, for a young woman who excels in basketball— and by spreading her positive perspective on what it means to be beautiful and successful.

"When I was younger, I watched a lot of TV. I knew everything about actresses and stars, and lots of my friends were into models and trying to look like them. But I grew up in a single-parent home. I saw my mom's struggles and I knew there wasn't going to be a lot of money for me to go to college, which was something that I really wanted to do. So it was pretty easy to not get too caught up in glamour and to stay grounded. Staying active in sports totally kept me from getting starstruck. I hung out mostly with athletes who appreciated their bodies for what they could do, not just how they looked. That helped keep me from getting obsessed with my image.

Beauty *Plus* Success

Plus-sized stars are becoming as well known as their thin counterparts. Mia Tyler (half sister of actress Liv) wears a size twelve through sixteen, depending on the brand, and has appeared in *Vogue, Seventeen,* and ad campaigns for the hip European clothing store H&M. Model Emme and actresses Kathy Najimy and Camryn Manheim are also helping change the face of beauty and success. Even *America's Next Top Model* has featured plus-sized contestants.

"The media put out what sells, but we shouldn't let them dictate who we are or how we feel about ourselves. We shouldn't sell ourselves short just because they're putting women in magazines that might not look like us. We complain about skinny models, but we don't have to buy the magazines! If we want to see someone of a different ethnicity or body type, then let's let our voices be heard. I think it's time to start standing up for things that we believe in and just get it done.

"I have so many different scratches and bumps on my body from sports, but that doesn't make me less beautiful. Every mark on me is there for a reason and has a story behind it. We can't depend on other people and things to tell us we're beautiful. We're all beautiful in different ways. And having a strong connection with yourself is what lets you be confident and walk with your head high—no matter what's out there."

Ariel Fox, founder of Sticker Sisters

When Ariel, twenty-four, was thirteen, she wasn't into the pop music, magazine reading, and shopping that interested most of her classmates. She started reading

'zines instead, where she came across an announcement from two girls who were making stickers that used positive characters from children's books like *Eloise* and *Pippi Longstocking* to put out empowering messages for girls on stickers and T-shirts. Ariel placed an order, but sadly her stickers never arrived in the mail. Her disappointment got her thinking that if she wanted something sporting a positive, pro-girl message, other girls probably did, too. So she decided to just make them herself.

Living Large(r)

Mannequins, most often made in sizes two or four, are now frequently being manufactured in size eight and above. That's still smaller than most women, but, hey, it's a start. The hips and thighs are being made to look more round and real than flat and fake.

"When I was younger, I tried really hard to be into the same things other girls were, but it just wasn't me. I didn't connect with most people at school. I had been thinking about writing my own 'zine about stuff that interested me, but after my sticker order didn't arrive, I thought my time could be better spent making something that other people also wanted.

"I started really small. I sat down at my computer and designed four cool stickers to start with that said things like "Girls Can Do Anything," "Girl Power," "Punk Rock Isn't Just for Your Boyfriend," and "Visit Our Power Room." Then I printed them out on sticker labels and made a flyer that announced my new venture, which I mailed to about thirty people who wrote 'zines, They started passing them out to people and writing about me, and word just spread.

"One time, this all-female band that plays at women's prisons ordered a bunch of stickers to decorate their instruments with inspirational messages. And another time I was at a Le Tigre concert, and I noticed a girl who was wearing shoelaces I designed that said "Action Not Glamour." I told her that I created them, but I'm not sure she believed me because I was so young. It didn't matter though, because it was so cool that she was helping spread my message!

"I used to wonder if there was still a need for something like stickers with a message, because for a few years it seemed like everything was about girl power. That's faded a little now, but are things really that much better for girls? There's still so much to be done so Sticker Sisters is branching out into things like Band-Aids, which are called "Brave Girl Aids" and

T-shirts. Sticker Sisters has taught me that we really can do whatever we want. We don't have to just sit there and passively accept what pop culture feeds us. We can create something different. Hey, I got started with ten bucks and my computer."

GoVeg.com, activist at People for the Ethical Treatment of Animals (PETA)

In March 2003, Karin Robertson legally changed her name to GoVeg.com so she could help get the word out about becoming vegetarian all the time, like whenever she introduces herself, or when someone calls out her name across a crowded room, or she signs a check to pay her rent. Today, twenty-four-year-old "GoVeg" (as she's known to family and friends) is the director of the Fish Empathy project at People for the Ethical Treatment of Animals (PETA). GoVeg.com admits that some people laugh or are shocked when they find out her name, but she's happy with her decision because she never misses a chance to educate people about the plight of animals that are raised for food.

"When I was in tenth grade, I did a research paper on cosmetic companies and animal testing. I came across information about Factory Farms and couldn't believe the horrible conditions pigs and chickens and other animals were raised in just to be eaten. I decided right then that I was never going to eat another animal.

I'm from the Midwest, where there are lots of cattle farms, and I never met another vegetarian while growing up. I didn't have any role models. But a friend of mine was changing her name after getting a divorce, and I came up with the idea of changing my own name to encourage more people to learn about vegetarianism. Simple things like opening a bank account or going through airport security have become harder because people think I'm joking when I tell them my name is GoVeg.com. Everywhere I go, I carry around the official document showing that I have changed my name. But it's astonishing how many e-mails I have gotten saying 'Thanks so much for changing your name. I checked out the site and became vegetarian!' That makes it worth it. I hope my actions help others realize that they can help animals full-time, not just as a hobby or something that is fun to do on the weekends.

"In my opinion, it doesn't matter what a person looks like. It matters how dedicated she is to something. And really important people, those who have changed my perspective on things, I couldn't even begin to tell you what they looked like! When I'm old and wrinkly, I think it's going to be more important to look back and say, 'Geez, I really *did* something with my life!' than to know I always looked good."

Camilla Bradley, fashion designer, owner of CK Bradley boutiques

Back when Camilla Bradley, twenty-nine, was a college senior, she would sit on the main quad of her New England campus and make personalized ribbon belts for fellow students. They were such a hit she added tote

bags, small purses, and cheerful, brightly colored clothing to her repertoire. Today her products are sold at over four hundred shops nationwide, and she owns boutiques in New York City, Virginia, and Rhode Island. Her accessories and clothes have been featured in major fashion magazines like *In Style, Marie Claire*, and *Teen Vogue*, but Camilla *always* makes sure to keep it real.

"When I was fifteen, I wanted to be a model *so* badly. I mean, who doesn't want to be just like all the women and girls who are held up as ideals? So I gave it a shot, and even landed a really well known agent in New York

A Milkshake a Day . . .

Israel's top fashion photographer, Adi Barkan, thinks images of skinny models contribute to eating disorders like anorexia and bulimia in teen girls. That's why he launched the "Look Good and Stay Alive" campaign, which asks advertisers like clothing chains and food manufacturers to use only models who have a body mass index (BMI)—a height to fat ratio—of at least 19. Healthy young adults normally have a BMI between 18.5 and 24.9. Serious anorexics can be as low as 7, while underweight teens are usually at about 13 or 14. At open auditions, Barkan often tells hopefuls with potential to come back after gaining—not losing—weight, and he says he won't give up until he persuades top fashion designers like Calvin Klein to join the campaign. Isn't it great when people throw their weight around for the right reasons?

City. Then my agency told me I'd have to lose eight pounds, which was crazy because I was the skinniest girl in my class. But I did it, anyway.

"After a few years though, the modeling wasn't really taking off. And my father kept encouraging me to do something different—to stand out—which I started doing through playing sports and getting involved in art. Looking back, I think the real reason I wanted to model was to get noticed. When I got to college, everyone dressed the same way, and I really wanted to differentiate myself. I would shop at the same places in the mall as other girls, but then I'd sew on red ribbons to the cuffs of my pants, or add some special touch—and *everyone* would notice and compliment me.

"Sometimes I felt pretty uncool sitting around my dorm room sewing. That's what grandmothers do. But people liked my designs and started ordering them for their parents and friends, and that gave me a lot of confidence. I started to see how much better it was to be known for things that I am good at instead of how I look.

"A public relations firm I hired once CK Bradley started to take off told me that I *had* to get celebrities to wear my clothing so that the brand would get more recognition. But I'm not into that kind of hype. I make clothes for real people. I've never hired models for ad campaigns because I want customers to see *real* bodies in my clothes in *real* situations. I've also never hired a fit model because they're paid hundreds of dollars an hour to maintain a perfect body. They don't have the same hips and shape as real young women. I design for the girl who has a stomach and breasts—so that she can put on one of my dresses and feel gorgeous. Because there is nothing better than wearing a dress that you can do everything you want in, from cartwheels to flips on the dance floor to eating all the food you want, and still look good and feel comfortable!"

Yi Shun Lai, triathlete and founder of Divas in the Dirt

Yi Shun, thirty, was a totally normal teen. When she looked at magazines and TV shows, she simultaneously wanted to be like all the perfect girls she saw, and she hated how one-sided they seemed to be. She was annoyed by how the media make it seem like if you were pretty, you couldn't be into hard-core sports—and how if you were a jock, you couldn't also be considered hot. So she created a Web community for sporty girls and young women who want to prove that they can be more than what the media dictates.

"Whether we realize it or not, most of us are starstruck. Everyone wants to be as thin and beautiful as the stars that get attention and glory. Like a lot of mothers, my mom always encouraged me to be slim and pretty. I don't think it was because she was obsessed with weight, but because she, too, realized what type of girls got all the praise, and she wanted that for me.

"As a teen, I wanted to look good, but I didn't always have a lot of confidence in my body. Sports like track and field and skiing helped turn that around. When I read teen magazines, I skimmed the beauty and fashion articles because I was really more interested in the profiles about girls who rode BMX bikes or who played football. They were usually kind of like me: sporty, but into other things as well. They made me feel good about myself.

"Once I got a little older, I couldn't find enough role models in the media who were like me: a girl who likes to be athletically adventurous and get dirty but who also likes to be a little glam. That's why I founded Divas in the Dirt. I wanted to create a Web community for young women who want to get into sports but who also like to get gorgeous—because we can do both! Being pretty is fun, but depending on appearance for one's inner confidence isn't the way to go. There are so many great rewards and benefits to be found in other parts of life. Besides, strength and confidence in one's body *are* beautiful. Beauty isn't about body measurement and weight, it's about the amazing things your body and soul can do."

How to Be a Real Role Model

You might not realize it, but you're probably a role

model to someone you know. Maybe it's for your athletic skills or your ability to get along with everyone. Perhaps it's because you're a great public speaker or always make time to help a friend in need. Either way, it's a great chance to be a role model who has more to offer than "the look" or a label. So remember to:

☆ Stand up for what you believe in, even if it's not hip or trendy
☆ Be honest with yourself and others, but always in a kind way
☆ Make an effort to understand and respect others' opinions, which might be different from yours
☆ Make a difference
☆ Help others more than you help yourself
☆ Be willing to listen to ideas that are different from yours
☆ Treat all people equally
☆ Stick with a task until it's done—and done well
☆ Work as a team player
☆ Honor your commitments

More and more, there's an understanding that all the status and hype showered on celebrities is misplaced and should be spread to other accomplished women. Help things along by talking up the girls and women you think deserve to be recognized for their work and personality—and by being a living example of the changes you think are important.

BACK TALK BLOG

☆ Who are your role models?

☆ Are your role models amazing women like your mother or a teacher?

☆ Have you found real role models in the media that inspire you?

☆ What sort of role models do you wish were celebrated by the media?

☆ What qualities do you think a role model should have?

☆ Dish on the blog.

chapter seven

Let's Celebrate!

Now that you know what's real and what's made up, you have the power to walk away from the hype and shine the spotlight on real beauty. Not sure how to do that? Following are some suggestions.

Help Others See Through the Hype

1. Collect images of stars and celebrities and images of other women who have done amazing things. (Find images and biographical information about accomplished historical and contemporary female

icons at the National Women's History Project at www.nwhp.org.) Gather a group of family or friends and invite them to call out the names of the women they recognize as you hold up the images. If they have an easier time naming stars than other women, teach them a little about celebrity hype!

2. Buy a women's or teen magazine. Rip out each page and place it in one of two piles. In the first pile, place articles and images that reinforce being starstruck, such as behind-the-scenes information about star's lives, red carpet photos, advertisements, and fashion spreads that show stars and women who have "the look" or women who look like them. In the second pile place all the ads and articles that show alternative ideas of female success and beauty. Which pile is bigger? Discuss the ultimate message of the magazine. Ask your teacher if

you can make a presentation for credit in social studies, history, or civics class.

3. Get a group of friends together and give everyone two index cards. On one card, have them list the names of three celebrities they like, then flip it over and write down what they do (actress, model, star athlete). On the second card, have them list the three professions they think are important (e.g., doctor, mother, lawyer, judge). Then ask them to flip over the card and write down the name of a famous woman in each of those professions. Which card took longer to complete? What does it say about who the most recognizable women in the world are?

4. Make a list together with a group of friends about the qualities that you think should define beauty and success. Write down the traits your friends call out, like caring, dedicated, creative. Then pick a fashion magazine at random and go through the

ads and articles. How many images and articles can you find that support the characteristics on your list?

5. Throw a party for a few friends and write down the following questions on pieces of paper before tossing them into a hat. Ask each girl to draw one and give her answer. Be supportive of each other, because if one of you is experiencing a certain feeling, others might be, too. Feel free to make up your own questions or use these:

☆ How do you define beauty?

☆ Do you consider yourself beautiful?

☆ What feelings toward your body do you have most often?

☆ If you could change something about your body, what would it be? What effect do you think it would have on your life, and where do you think your desire to change something comes from?

☆ What makes you feel most beautiful?

☆ How do you feel when you see a girl who has "the look"?

☆ How do you feel when guys go crazy over stars?

Dream Positive

Before going to sleep one night, try to remember all the moments during the day when you felt good about your body (like during gym class, at sports practice, or when buying a new pair of great-fitting jeans). Then recall the occasions when you felt bad about or ashamed of your body. Fall asleep focusing on the good thoughts and letting go of all the criticisms or judgments.

Keep a Hype Journal

Jot down all the examples of messages that aim to keep us starstruck. Briefly describe what the ads look like or what a company's slogan is. Flip back through the journal occasionally to see the similarities among the messages.

Surround Yourself with Real People

It can be hard to change your thinking when you spend most of your time with people who buy into the media's definitions of female beauty and success. You don't have to pull away from friends who do that, but try adding in some new ones that are more aware of media influence, and who are doing their own thing.

Throw Starstruck Thoughts in the Trash

Write down the doubts and dissatisfaction that result from celebrity hype—things like "I can't help wishing that I looked more like the stars of my favorite TV show" or "Why can't my stomach be as flat as all the girls on the red carpet?" Then crumple up the paper and toss it in the trash . . . because now you know better.

Create Inspiring Stickers

Head to an office supply store to buy a pack of blank self-adhesive labels and some colorful markers, or sit down at your computer to whip up stickers with phrases like:

Get Real!
This vision of beauty is not reality.
Women should be valued for more than looking good in a bikini.

Airbrushing does not equal beauty.
Beauty comes in all shapes and colors.
Who says this is beautiful?
Sexiness is being yourself.
Be your own role model.

Or make up your own sayings. Cover your school notebooks or locker with hyped-up ads, then place your stickers on top.

Challenge Yourself

Time spent talking about how great celebs look, which diets they're on, and all that, could be spent making changes! So instead of wasting time trying to get "the look," try writing a poem, learning to mountain climb, or improving your grades. In the long run, skills—not appearance—will pay off and make you self-fulfilled.

Express Your Opinions

Speak out if you don't like what you see in the media. Write letters to magazine editors or movie studios. Or create a petition against a particular ad, slogan, or image that values "the look" over women's other qualities. Collect signatures and send them to the responsible company or magazine.

Create a Playlist

When you find a singer or band that's putting out a positive message, buy their songs online and burn your favorites onto a CD. Search for the lyrics online or copy them down yourself, then include them as inspirational liner notes when you give the CDs to friends as gifts. Consider including old favorites like

"I Will Survive" by Gloria Gaynor
"32 Flavors" by Alana Davis
"Beautiful" by Christina Aguilera
"Just a Girl" by No Doubt
"Respect" by Aretha Franklin
"We Are Family" by Sister Sledge

"Can't Hold Us Down" by Christina Aguilera and
  Lil' Kim
"Expression" by Salt-N-Pepa
"Hat 2 Da Back" by TLC

And almost anything by Tori Amos, Ani DiFranco, Le
Tigre, Sarah McLachlan, the Indigo Girls, Shawn
Colvin, and Queen Latifah. Share your list on the
blog!

And the Award for Best Lyrics Goes To . . .

India Arie's grammy-nominated hit "Video." Just check out the amazing chorus:

I'm not the average girl from your video

And I ain't built like a supermodel

But I learned to love myself unconditionally

Because I am a queen

I'm not the average girl from your video

My worth is not determined by the price of my clothes

No matter what I'm wearing I will always be India Arie

Create a Screensaver

Scan in or grab unrealistic images, then add on your
own captions before uploading them to your computer's desktop. It'll get your message out whenever
you take a break.

Produce a 'Zine

Compose an essay or two about experiences that have

made you question celebrity hype and unrealistic beauty standards. Interview some real role models and add in quotes from your friends and family. Ask an artist friend to draw some positive images, then photocopy your masterpiece at a copy shop or at your parents' office and distribute! Ask for contributions for your next issue from people who give you good feedback.

Have a Media-Free Week

Go cold turkey on the media for a few days. Turn off the TV. Give up glossy magazines and surfing the net. Keep a journal about how you end up spending your time. Reread your favorite book and mark up all the best passages. Plan a fun activity to do during the time you'd normally zone out online. Act like a tourist in your own town and rediscover the best it has to offer.

Chat Up Real Role Models

Talk to older girls and women about their definitions of beauty and success. Ask your grandmother if she felt pressured to look like ideals created by advertisers and the media.

Fund Your Own Media Project

Head to the Listen Up Youth Media Network (www.pbs.org/merrow/listenup/) and check out the "Call for Entries" channel to find out about contests and festivals open to nationwide participation. Click on the "Funding" channel to link to organizations that make money available to young people who create their own media.

There are tons of possibilities for making change—

so get creative and *have fun* while you raise awareness about what's real and what's hype. And although it can seem like your individual actions don't matter, they do! So keep it up, because you never know who's listening—and who really needs to hear what you have to say. Your words and ideas might just inspire someone else to get involved, too.

 BACK TALK BLOG

☆ Your conversations, choices, and ideas are more influential than you realize. They might spark a plan or a chain reaction without your ever even knowing. So do your thing and share your experiences on your blog. And make sure to post about your own creative strategies for helping others see through the hype.

Afterword

Beyond the Hype . . .

It took me a really long time to understand that while models and stars *are* very beautiful and successful, and while it *would* be cool to be like them, my dreams of being like them and my unconditional respect for them were a result of what I had seen in the media.

But working both in front of the camera and behind the scenes showed me that today's definitions of female success and beauty are created by powerful entities that are more concerned with selling their products than with our self-esteem and future goals. Heck, most would actually *prefer* us to feel crappy about ourselves and want to be like everything we see on TV and in magazines because it means more sales for them. I've also learned that these messages are so strong that they affect everyone (whether or not you dream of being discovered, like I did) and that there are many more definitions of beauty and success than are shown in movies, magazines, and advertisements.

Making a difference might seem impossible, but it's not. The first step is learning where the hype comes from and how to recognize real beauty, which you've already done by reading this book. The next step is sharing what you've learned—so that women and girls of *all* looks and talents come to be celebrated as beautiful and successful.

Resources

For Teens

Magazines

Teen Voices: You're More Than Just a Pretty Face
  (www.teen-voices.com)
New Moon: The Magazine for Girls and Their Dreams
  (www.newmoon.org)

Organizations and Web sites:

· **Go Ask Alice** (www.goaskalice.com): Reliable, honest information about sex, bodies, and relationships
· **Teen Wire** (www.teenwire.com): Honest, nonjudgmental information about sexuality and health
· **About-Face** (www.about-face.org): Self-esteem for women of all
  ages sizes, races, and backgrounds through media education,
  outreach, and activism
· **Girls Inc** (www.girlsinc.org/gc/): Smart games, surveys, and ob-
  servations to get girls thinking
· **For Girls and Their Dreams** (www.forgirlsandtheirdreams.org):
  Pen pals, book clubs, info about girls around the world
· **Just Think** (www.justhink.org): Teaching young people to under-
  stand the words and images in media and to think for themselves
· **Young People's Press** (www.ypp.net): News from a youth

perspective

- **Don't Buy It** (www.pbskids.org/dontbuyit): How the media operate and the importance of consuming a healthy media diet
- **Sticker Sisters** (www.stickersisters.com): Shoelaces, stickers, and more with sassy sayings
- **Something Fishy** (www.something-fishy.org): Support for people with eating disorders and their loved ones
- **The Eating Disorders Information Network** (www.edinga. org): Committed to preventing eating disorders
- **Fuzzy Feet** (www.fuzzyfeet.org): Delivering new slippers to hospitals to help sick kids and teens feel loved
- **CK Bradley** (www.ckbradley.com): Preppy clothes *by* a real girl *for* other real girls

Books

Dee, Catherine. *The Girls' Guide to Life: Take Charge of Your Personal Life, Your School Time, Your Social Scene, and Much More!* New York: Little, Brown and Company, 2005.

Devillers, Julia. *GirlWise: How to Be Confident, Capable, Cool, and in Control.* New York: Three Rivers Press, 2002.

Drill, Esther, Heather McDonald, and Rebecca Odes. *Deal with It.* New York: Pocket Books, 1999.

Drill, Esther, Heather McDonald, and Rebecca Odes. *The Looks Book.* New York: Penguin Books, 2002.

Edut, Ophira, ed. *Body Outlaws: Young Women Write About Body Image and Identity.* Emeryville, Calif.: Seal Press, 2000

Findlen, Barbara, ed. *Listen UP: Voices from the Next Feminist Generation.* Emeryville, Calif: Seal Press, 1995.

Gottlieb, Lori. *Stick Figure: A Diary of My Former Self.* New York: The Berkley Publishing Group, 2001.

Gowen, L. Kris. *Image and Identity: Becoming the Person You Are.* Lanham, MD: Scarecrow Press, 2005.

Mackler, Carolyn. *The Earth, My Butt, and Other Big Round Things.* Cambridge, Mass.: Candlewick Press, 2003.

Mackler, Carolyn. *Love and Other Four Letter Words.* New York: Laurel Leaf, 2002.

Mackler, Carolyn. *Vegan Virgin Valentine.* Cambridge, Mass:
Candlewick Press, 2004.

Weiner, *Jessica. A Very Hungry Girl: How I Filled Up on Life and You Can Too.*
Carlsbad, Calif.: Hay House, 2003.

Schwager, Tina. *Gutsy Girls: Young Women Who Dare.* Minneapolis: Free
Spirit Press, 1999.

Shandler, Sara, ed. *Ophelia Speaks: Adolescent Girls Write About Their Search
for Self.* New York: HarperCollins, 1999.

Weston, Carol. *For Teens Only: Quotes, Notes, & Advice You Can Use.* New
York: Harper Trophy, 2002.

For Adults

Magazines

Bust: For Women with Something to Get off Their Chests (www.bust.com)
Bitch: The Feminist Response to Pop Culture (www.bitchmagazine.com)
Ms. (www.msmagazine.com)

Organizations and Web sites

· **Mind on the Media** (www.motm.org): Inspiring independent
thinking and fostering critical analysis of media messages
· **Girls Women + Media project** (www.mediaandwomen.org):
Working to increase awareness of how pop culture and media
represent, affect, employ, and serve girls and women
· **Girls Inc** (www.girlsinc.org): Inspiring girls to be strong, smart,
and bold; Web site includes contact information for local chapters
· **The Media Education Foundation** (www.mediaed.org): The
premier resource for educational videos on media literacy and
youth culture
· **Media Watch** (www.mediawatch.com): Challenging racism, sex-
ism, and violence in the media through education and action
· **The Action Coalition for Media Education**
(www.amecoalition.org): A network of media educators, health
advocates, media reformers, independent media makers, and
community organizers

- **Campaign for a Commercial-Free Childhood (CCFC)** (www.commercialexploitation.org): A group against the corporate manipulation of young people
- **The Empower Program** (www.empowered.org): Working with youth to end the culture of violence
- **Divas in the Dirt** (www.divasinthedirt.com): A Web community by and for women who like to get dirty playing adventure sports but who are in touch with their inner girly girls
- **Bad Ads** (www.badads.org): A blog about the danger of advertisements creeping into every aspect of daily life

Books

Baumgardner, Jennifer and Amy Richards. *Grassroots: A Field Guide for Feminist Activism.* New York: Farrar Straus Giroux, 2005

Baumgardner, Jennifer and Amy Richards. *Manifesta: Young Women, Feminism, and the Future.* New York: Farrar Straus Giroux, 2000.

Kelly, Joe. *Dads and Daughters: How to Inspire, Understand, and Support Your Daughter When She's Growing Up So Fast.* New York: Broadway Books, 2002.

Kilbourne, Jean. *Can't Buy My Love: How Advertising Changes the Way We Think and Feel.* New York: Touchstone Books, 1999.

Gruver, Nancy. *How to Say It to Girls: Communicating with Your Growing Daughter.* New York: The Berkley Publishing Group, 2004.

Linn, Susan. *Consuming Kids: The Hostile Takeover of Childhood.* New York: The New Press, 2004.

Maine, Margo and Joe Kelley. *The Body Myth: Adult Women and the Pressure to be Perfect.* Hoboken, NJ: John Wiley & Sons, 2005

Maine, Margo. *Body Wars: Making Peace with Women's Bodies—An Activist's Guide.* Carlsbad, Calif: Gürze Books, 2000.

Quart, Alyssa. *Branded: The Buying and Selling of Teenagers.* New York: Perseus Publishing, 2003.

Pipher, Mary. *Reviving Ophelia: Saving the Selves of Adolescent Girls.* New York: Ballantine, 1995.

Pollack, William. *Real Boys: Rescuing Our Sons from the Myths of Boyhood.* New York: Random House, 1998.

Schor, Juliet. *Born to Buy: The Commercialized Child and the New Consumer*

Culture. New York: Scribner, 2004.

Tanenbaum, Leora. *Catfight: Rivalries Among Women: From Diets to Dating, from the Boardroom to the Delivery Room.* New York: Perennial, 2003.

Tanenbaum, Leora. *Slut: Growing Up Female with a Bad Reputation.* New York: Perennial, 2000.

Wolf, Naomi. *The Beauty Myth: How Images of Beauty Are Used Against Women.* New York: Perennial, 2001.

Video/Film/TV (available at many libraries, colleges, and universities)

I Am Beautiful. A documentary film featuring actress Courteney Cox Arquette, country singer Trisha Yearwood, producer Linda Ellerbee, and activist Gloria Steinem. Available through the Esteemed Woman Foundation (www.esteemedwoman.com).

The Merchants of Cool: A Report on the Creators and Marketers of Popular Culture for Teenagers. 2002. A PBS/Frontline documentary. (shoppbs.org).

Soft Sell: The Image of Women on Television. 1989. Produced by Media Watch, Toronto, Canada.

Killing Us Softly 3. Advertising's Image of Women. 2000. Jean Kilbourne. Produced by the Media Education Foundation, Northampton, Massachusetts, 1-800-897-0089 (www.mediaed.org).

Slim Hopes: Advertising and the Obsession with Thinness. 1995. Jean Kilbourne. Produced by the Media Education Foundation, Northampton, Massachusetts, 1-800-897-0089 (www.mediaed.org).

Tough Guise: Violence Media and the Crisis in Masculinity. 1999. Jackson Katz. Directed by Sut Jhally. Produced by the Media Education Foundation, Northampton, Massachusetts, 1-800-897-0089 (www.mediaed.org).

Recovering Bodies: Overcoming Eating Disorders. 1997. Katherine Sender and Sanjay Talreja. Produced by the Media Education Foundation, Northampton, Massachusetts, 1-800-897-0089 (www.mediaed.org).

Behind the Screens: Hollywood Goes Hypercommercial. 2000. Matt Soar &

Susan Ericsson. Produced by the Media Education Foundation, Northampton, Massachusetts, 1-800-897-0089 (www.mediaed.org).

Notes

14   *John Robert Powers opens the world's first modeling agency.* Michael Gross, *Model: The Ugly Business of Beautiful Women* (New York: William Morrow and Company, 1995), 10, 34, 36.

14   *Models use only their first name.* Ibid, 40.

14   *Models earn $25.* Ibid, 37

15   *The owner of a small modeling agency coins the term* supermodel. Ibid, 12.

15   *"Model hounds."* Ibid, 61.

15   *Models start to become accepted into society.* Ibid, 138.

15   *Modeling's first international star.* Ibid, 179–83.

16   *English Boy calls its clients "not just models, but model people."* Ibid, 175, 229.

16   *John Casablancas establishes Elite Model Management.* Elite.com

16   *Cheryl Tiegs, an American model from California.* Ibid, 242, 331, 335.

17   *Claudia Schiffer is discovered.* Gross, 475, 477.

19   *Victoria's Secret fashion show broadcast on the Web.* "Victoria's Secret Drops TV Show," CBSNews.com, April 13, 2004.

21   *Fashion modeling and prostitution are the only careers in which women consistently earn more.* Naomi Wolf, *The Beauty Myth* (Canada: Vintage Canada, 1997), 49–50.

22   *Number of female judges, lawyers, doctors, engineers, and elected officials exploded.* Ibid, 25.

23   *Cultural obsession with women's appearance.* Ibid, 28.

23   *Tatiana Patitz, who's modeled for* Vogue. Arthur Elgort, *Arthur Elgort's Models Manual* (New York: Grand Street Press, 1993), 67.

23 *Supermodel Linda Evangelista.* Gross, *Model,* 437.

23 *Veronica Webb, former Revlon spokesmodel.* Ibid, 448.

24 *She demands her dressing room have white flowers.* From "Sharon Stone demands filmmakers agree to a five-page list of perks" archives, the smokinggun.com.

27 *Quotes from real girls.* All quotes from girls are from telephone and e-mail interviews with the author or from posts to the author's former Web site, www.cultureofmodeling.com.

28 *Dreamers and Wannabees.* Maureen Maher, "Yoanna Be a Model," CBSnews.com, August 6, 2004.

41 *Percentage of teens going online every day.* Statistics from "Facts and Figures About Our TV Habit," TV-Turnoff Network, November 2005 and AOL Digital Marketing Services and BuzzBack Market Research, cited at ketchum.com/DisplayWebPage/0,1,0032699,00.html.

41 *Profits the video game industry.* "Console Wars II: The Battle for Mainstream" Research and Market reports, www.researchandmarkets.com/reports/c3558/ cited in news release titled "New report claims the average American spent 75 hours in 2003 playing video games," September 10, 2004, Gamewinners.com.

43 *Images and messages appear and disappear.* "The Ad and the Ego," official study guide, robwilliamsmedia.com.

44 *"Buzz" and "Stealth" Marketing.* Juliet B. Schor, *Born to Buy: The Commercialized Child and the New Consumer Culture* (New York: Scribner 2004), 22.

46 *ABCs of Selling Stuff to Kids.* Campaign for a Commercial-Free Childhood, www.commercialfreechildhood.org and Noel C. Paul, "Branded for Life?" *Christian Science Monitor,* April 1, 2002.

46 *They secretly videotape kids in toy stores.* Schor, *Born to Buy,* 103.

47 *Digital Enhancement.* George Rush and Joanna Malloy, "The Unkindest Cut 'N' Paste for Julia," *The New York Daily News,* June 8, 2003.

48 *He'll create a flawless cover image.* Kate Betts, "The Man Who Makes the Pictures Perfect," *The New York Times,* February

2, 2003.

49   *Magazine editors can't always print everything they want.* Gloria
Steinem, "Sex, Lies & Advertising," *Ms.*, July/August 1990.

62   *Kim Basinger and Madonna have all hired body doubles.*
ShelleyMichelle.com.

62   *Winners of the Miss America pageants have had body mass indexes or BMI
considered "malnourished."* Journal of the American Medical Association.
(JAMA) March 2000. Normal, average women have a body
fat percentage of 20 to 25, while recent Miss America Winners have less than 18.5%, the WHO's base for malnutri-
tion.

64   *Which is ironic, since she isn't considered particularly attractive by most
Nigerians.* Norimitsu Onishi, "Globalization of Beauty
Makes Slimness Trendy," *New York Times,* Thursday, October
3, 2002.

64   *TV was introduced to the Pacific island nation of Fiji.* "Sharp Rise in
Eating Disorders in Fiji Follows Arrival of TV," press re-
lease, Harvard Medical School Office of Public Affairs,
May 17, 1999.

64   *The world spends $38 billion on hair-care.* "Pots of Promise," *The
Economist,* May 22, 2003.

66   *Breast implants jumped nearly threefold.* Jodi Mailander Farrell,
"More Teens Are Getting Breast Implants," *Stamford Advocate,* February 25, 2005, M4.

66   *Nicknamed "Dr. Boobner" because he performs an average of five implant
surgeries a day.* From "50 Most Loathsome New Yorkers," *New
York Press,* March 30–April 5, 2005, 16, and Farrell, *Stamford
Advocate.*

66   *Actress Demi Moore reportedly had a $400,000 total-body makeover.*
As reported on the Internet Movie Database (imdb.com)
on November 15, 2002.

67   *American Society of Plastic Surgeons thinks extreme makeover television
shows and celebrity look-alike contests contribute.* Kathleen Doheny,
"Plastic Surgery Not Just for Wealthy Anymore," August
30, 2005, Health on the Net Foundation,
www.hon.ch/News/HSN/527699.html.

68   *59% of teen girls are reportedly dissatisfied with their body.* Pediatrics. "Exposure to the Mass Media and Weight Concerns Among Girls," March 1999.

68   *Some girls are more afraid of becoming fat than they are of nuclear war.* 1996 Council on Size and Weight Discrimination, pg 1. Referenced at http://www.ejhs.org/volume5/Areton/ 03Background.htm.

70   *Teen dies from heart failure after following low carb diet.* Philip Recchia, "Her Battle of Bulge Is Fatal for Teenager Doing Atkins," *New York Post,* August 24, 2003.

71   *Ironically, thinness has become the symbol of beauty at a time when nearly one-third of American adults over the age of 20 are obese.* Statistics from the Centers for Disease Control and Prevention as of Summer 2005.

71   *Americans suffer from eating disorders and approximately 90 percent of them are young women.* Jennifer Daw, "Eating Disorders on the Rise: A Capitol Hill Briefing Calls Attention to Eating Disorders," *Monitor on Psychology,* Volume 32, No. 9 (October 2001).

71   *Average age of sufferers is dropping rapidly.* Laura Landro, "Eating Disorders on the Rise: Sufferers Are Getting Younger," *Wall Street Journal,* March 30, 2004.

80   *Guys watch more TV. Boys to Men: Messages About Masculinity.* A national poll of children, focus groups, and content analysis of entertainment media. Children Now, 1999.

81   *Men's shopping magazines, makeover reality shows, and spas.* See more in *Making Weight: Men's Conflicts with Food, Weight, Shape, and Appearance.* Anderson, A., L. Cohn and T. Holbrook. (Carlsbad, Calif: Gurze Books, 2000).

81   *For every three female cases, there's one male case. American Journal of Psychiatry* (2001) 158: 570–74.

81   *Out of more than 7.4 million plastic surgery procedures performed.* "Most Men View Cosmetic Plastic Surgery Positively," press release from the American Society of Plastic Surgeons, January 24, 2005.

81   *Boys watched a music video by Britney Spears.* EJ Mundell, "Sitcoms,

Videos Make Even Fifth-Graders Feel Fat" (August 26, 2002) as quoted in National Institute on Media and the Family Fact Sheet.

82   *Accomplishments are more important than their appearance.* From author interview with Jackson Katz, anti-sexist male activist and co-creator of Tough Guise: Violence, Media, and the Crisis in Masculinity (2000), an educational video produced by the Media Education Foundation.

84   *You don't sleep with a personality.* From the Ask Bradley column at Girlsandsports.com, http://www.girlsandsports.com/askbradley.php?id=23

97   *Actress Kate Winslet, who's always been honest about being comfortable with her body naturally.* Tony Parsons, themirror.co.uk, January 13, 2003.

113   *He launched the "Look Good and Stay Alive," campaign.* Ian Mackinnon, "Model Purge on Anorexics Makes Weight Vital Statistic." *The Times,* December 31, 2004.

Audrey D. Brashich has worked for teen and women's magazines for over ten years. Her work has appeared in *Teen People*, *YM*, *Sassy*, *Elle Girl*, *Cosmo Girl*, *Shape*, *Ms.*, *Health*, and many others. She has a master's degree in American studies from Brown University, where she focused on the history of popular culture and gender studies. Audrey writes regularly about media literacy and body image.

Shawn Banner went to Oberlin College and the Fashion Institute of Technology and recently got a masters in education from Sage. He says this project was perfect for him, because his mother is a great feminist, and his daughter is just at the age that this will matter to her. Shawn teaches elementary school in Saratoga Springs, New York, where he lives with his son and daughter.